BACKLASH

A Compendium of Lore and Lies
(Mostly Lies) Concerning Hunting,
Fishing and the Out of Doors

by

Galen Winter

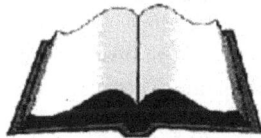

CCB Publishing
British Columbia, Canada

Backlash: A Compendium of Lore and Lies (Mostly Lies)
Concerning Hunting, Fishing and the Out of Doors

Copyright ©1993, 2000, 2011 by Galen Winter
ISBN-13   978-1-927360-07-1
Third Edition

Library and Archives Canada Cataloguing in Publication

Winter, Galen, 1926-
Backlash : a compendium of lore and lies (mostly lies) concerning hunting,
fishing and the out of doors / written by Galen Winter – 3rd ed.
Short stories.
ISBN 978-1-927360-07-1
Also available in electronic format.
I. Title.
PS3573.I565B33 2011   813'.54   C2011-907876-7

The stories contained herein were first published in *The Wisconsin Sportsman* and *The Wisconsin Outdoor Journal* magazines.

Publisher: CCB Publishing
              British Columbia, Canada
              www.ccbpublishing.com

Contents

Foreword

Gathered around the campfire on a cool October evening are four drowsy grouse hunters. Slouched on lawn chairs, chins on chests, they're yielding to the day's hunt, evening cocktails and plattersful of Grouse Breast Villa Louis. Soon they'll trudge off to tents and sleeping bags. For now, however, they quietly savor the final moments of a perfect day afield.

Beyond the shadows, busying himself with after-dinner kitchen chores, is the camp cook and self appointed poet laureate.

He stacks the last dish and, honoring a personal tradition, commences reciting "The Cremation of Sam McGee" with a booming eloquence. It is the first of a series of grouse camp poems he customarily recounts.

After several verses, however, he pauses to consider his inattentive audience. The oldest among them is his junior by ten years. Yet to a man they've caved in before the shank of the evening.

He pours himself another dollop of The Macallan and quietly approaches the ring of reposing comrades. Reaching into the pocket of his brush pants, he withdraws a handful of 20 gauge number eights and casually tosses them into the campfire. He sips his scotch and waits.

At the pop of the first primer, four heads snap erect. The following explosions send sparks and hunters flying in a confusion of shrieks and curses. "Perhaps," says the poet, "you'd prefer Kipling's Road to Mandalay?"

The moment was classic Winter. I've known the man for over a decade and can attest that his good humor is not confined to the printed page. He's demonstrated his mastery of the practical joke by making a fool of me from Hudson Bay goose camps to classic trout waters and points in between. Despite his stinging wit, or perhaps because of it, there's not a finer or funnier companion.

There's also a professional side to our long friendship. Many of the stories to follow first appeared in WISCONSIN SPORTSMAN - a magazine I owned and edited from 1972 until its sale in 1986. From its debut, Galen's BACKLASH column was a solid hit among readers. It was immediately obvious that here was a singular talent, not a McMannus or Zern wannabe.

His outrageous tales were usually centered within or near his beloved cabin along the South Branch of the Oconto River. It's here that Galen still regularly chases trout, grouse or deer. Often he will simply tinker with or relax in his impressive homemade sauna. In fact, I've long suspected that his bizarre story ideas are induced by prolonged exposure to steam heat (as I certainly know he is not a drug user).

For those who are reading Galen Winter for the first time, a word of warning: The author tends to dabble in social criticism.

This may be uncharted territory for most outdoor humorists, but Galen roams it freely, taking pot shots at politicians, militant feminists, anti-hunters and other pretentious prey too self-exalted for a little satire. All of this while spinning a package of first class hunting and fishing yarns at no extra charge.

So, settle in, head for the first story and expect the unexpected.

And don't take any of what's ahead too seriously. Galen certainly didn't.

Tom Petrie, Boulder Junction

Chapter One

The Sportsman

The Sportsman

The Little & Jones Webster Dictionary defines "Sportsman" as: A person possessing the qualities attributable to a sportsman; a chivalrous, fair minded person; one willing to incur and prepared to suffer defeat in fair competition without complaining.

I don't know who came up with that definition. You can bet your Thesaurus it wasn't anyone who hunts or fishes. There are some magnificent liars in our fraternity, but none so steeped in perjury that he could write such a preposterous statement.

Maybe some sportsmen, like pool sharks, crap shooters or basketball game bookies, could fit such a description, but if you are considering hunters and fishermen, it misses the mark and by a wide, wide margin.

Anyone who has suffered the defeat of spending a full day crashing through tag alders, blackberry bushes and swamps without sighting a woodcock or Ruffed Grouse can be expected to devote 75% of his evening campfire conversation denouncing the hunting, damning the local terrain and complaining bitterly about anything even vaguely associated with the hunt.

You can begin to commence to start to consider the possibility of a pheasant hunter being chivalrous and fair minded when he fires twice, misses and then says: "Good move there, bird. I hope we meet again next season." In real life, the ministers, ladies, children and, perhaps, career sailors home on leave would learn some new language if the actual comments make by the pheasant hunter were broadcast immediately after such a display of shooting.

If we limit the word to its application to hunters and fishermen, trying to define "sportsman" is a genuine test of vocabulary and imagination. It is a Herculean task similar to that of cleansing the Augean Stables. If you spend time associating with and listening to hunters and fishermen you will quickly develop the ability to recognize the material cleaned out of stables.

The outdoorsman is not like other people. Oh, I don't mean there's anything genetically distinctive about him. The differences seem to come, not from within, but from forces outside of him. As a class, hunters and fishers find themselves in situations where strange things happen.

It's as if some whimsical cosmic power enjoys frustrating and poking playful fun at the ones who love to hunt and fish. The Fates are constantly testing him, setting road blocks in his path and assailing him with 'the slings and arrows of outrageous fortune'. The fact that he, nevertheless, persevere in his avocation may be one of his major distinguishing characteristics.

Certainly, the outdoors type is not a heroic figure. Most of his endeavors are, at the very least, minor disasters. For every day he returns with an acceptable catch of legal sized trout, he will return on eight other days with nothing more than very wet trousers. For each day producing a limit of woodcock, four days will be spent looking for a lost dog. And the hunter who claims more deer kills than times he's been hopelessly lost in the woods is an Olympic class liar, a poor credit risk and probably a liberal.

The sportsman may appear to mellow with the years as does everyone else, but you need only scratch his surface and you'll find he has retained all the humor usually found in young men and the curiosity usually found in wives. Old outdoor types smile more. They don't know they're old. Polite society tends to treat the sportsman with caution, if not respect. They've got good reason to be skittish when he's around. They're not afraid he might use the wrong fork for the desert. What makes them tremble and panic is the fear that he might grab it with both hands and eat it the way he does at deer camp. He might do so just to see the look on the hostess' face.

The dedicated hunter/fisherman is courageous and doesn't hesitate to step out into the unknown if the act has any reasonable chance of furthering his enjoyment of the outdoor world. This is another way of saying he is foolhardy. Few entirely rational people will get into a leaky skiff at 5:00 a.m. and break ice to paddle a half mile through two foot waves in order to sit in a blind in sub-zero temperature in the hope of being able to entice a bluebill into gun range - and when the stratagem is successful, the hunter may very well miss.

If sanity is your game, stay away from trout streams on the opening day of the fishing season. It's hard to justify trout fishing during a snow storm, but the sportsman doesn't have a suspicion that such acts are anything but standard, usual and normal.

I don't know how to define "sportsman", but I know one when I see one. Here are six examples.

(NOTE: You have just been conned into reading the Author's Preface.)

Hypertension

Our astronomically knowledgeable associates advise us we experience the longest day of the year sometime around the 21st day of June. I don't know about you, but Jim Zimmerman is sure the longest day of the year was August 19th.

On that morning, his dreamless and serene sleep (experienced only by the innocent and pure of heart) was rudely interrupted by a pandemonium which, for a split second, convinced him he had somehow gotten himself into the center of an attack by the Valkyries.

He saw what might have been a whirling dervish swinging a turban sash. The sight and the tumult and the caterwauling that accompanied the scene not only called him abruptly into the wakened world, but also scared the hell out of him. No Wagnerian heroine nor Persian dervish, it was his wife, Carna, causing all the commotion.

The first words he could pick out were delivered at both a high velocity and decibel level. Here was his bride, pointing and shouting: "How did these get into your car?"

She'd discovered the pair of panty hose Clayton McHugh hid in Jim's fishing gear when he wasn't looking. Thinking fast, Jim answered: "Oh, you mean those experimental, extra-light, stocking foot waders?" It didn't do him a bit of good. His dream girl has absolutely no sense of humor when she is rattled.

From that auspicious beginning, Jim's day continued, every moment replete with a full measure of wrath, indignation and bile, occasionally lapsing into acrimony, rage and choler. Every modest inconsideration of which he may have been falsely accused during the previous thirty years was dredged up, dusted off and hurled at him.

He spent the whole day with an almost tangible apprehension that he was about to be physically assaulted. He jumped at every loud noise and there were many of them. To be on the safe side, he locked the gun cabinet and hid the shells and cartridges.

The moon had risen on that long, long day before Carna was finally convinced the panty hose must have been planted. She concluded (a) Jim wouldn't be that stupid; (b) he had a naturally honest look about him and, alternatively; (c) just maybe there was some truth in the story about them being left over from last fall when they were taken to the South Dakota hunt and intended to be used to carry pheasant specimen to the taxidermist without the risk of damaging their feathers.

With a calm and civilized atmosphere restored to the domicile, Jim's review of the events of that longest day of the year provoked a serious reflection on the pressures, hardships and adversities inflicted upon mankind simply because of the times in which we live.

Consider the extent to which our lives have been dislocated by that complicated series of yes/no switches we call the computer. A reservation clerk at the airlines may make an error all by himself and put an extra passenger or two on a flight. Give a computer a chance and it will try to put twice the capacity of the airplane on board.

Then there's that marvel of the age - television. Give any hardened criminal the choice and he will opt for capital punishment rather than be sentenced to ten years of watching TV commercials.

Ain't science wonderful? A generation ago we managed to

7

get by without cordless and mobile telephones which, each day, allow more people you don't want to talk to to talk to you. Some people, I am told, actually arrange to have telephones put into their cabins. Incredible!

Thanks to the development of modern technology and probably mega-dollar governmental grants over the last fifty years, fishermen have been able to advance from the use of split bamboo to steel, to fiber glass and to graphite boron fly rods. Now that we're friendly with China and can again get the right material, we are again able to make split bamboo fly rods.

Half the people in the country will die of some kind of heart problem. Now, due to advanced medical carpentry, we can give them sound transplanted hearts. Of course, we have to kill off the other half of the population in order to get the healthy hearts.

It's a tougher world than that of auld lang syne - that yesteryear before the sensibilities of the human race were deflowered by such things as the form of musical expression known as punk rock. It's no wonder the blood pressure, like Hemingway's sun, also rises. When I was a lad, life was much more comfortable. The stresses and complications of today were absent. It was a simpler time.

For example, there were mud turtles and snapping turtle and no other kinds of turtles to clutter up the genus. There were only two kinds of snakes - pine and grass. Pine snakes were long and black. Grass snakes weren't. Birds were a bit more complicated, but any small bird that wasn't a wren or yellow and, hence, a canary, was a sparrow. Anthropomorphism hadn't captured the hearts and minds of the non-sportsman.

(I apologize for that. You see, I've always wanted to use the word "anthropomorphism." I've also wanted to use the word "antidisestablishmentarianism." I suppose I'll never cause the word "antidisestablishmentarianism" to appear in print.)

In that simpler time, people died of old age, not hypertension. A duck stamp and a fishing license cost one dollar. A Chrysler cost $777, F.O.B. Detroit. A dozen decoys set you back $10. Today you can sell the same used blocks for $100 a copy.

They were halcyon times. Wisconsin had a fifteen duck per day bag limit and no unmanageable point system. The water in trout stream ran 9 degrees cooler. The hatches extended throughout the entire season. There were no aluminum beer cans marking deer stands. The racks on bucks were thick and heavy at the base. Pheasants' tails were all over 18 inches long.

What triggered the change from those happy times? What transformed our lives into this pressure tank, boiler factory existence? Was it the rise of Adolf Hitler? Or creeping socialism? Or the Department of Natural Recourses? No, friends, none of the above. According to Jim Zimmerman, the advent of stress and hypertension, the decay of ethical standards and the breakdown of time honored moral values all started with the invention of panty hose.

Wishing Won't Make It So

Doug Owen's wife collected things. She attended all flea markets and garage sales within a fifty mile radius of the homestead. Every auctioneer in the state knew her on a first name basis. It seemed like everything she bought went into the garage. It go so bad Doug had his choice of enlarging his home to accommodate all of the junk or throwing something away.

Doug sent his better half out of town so she wouldn't know what was happening, rolled up his sleeves and started cleaning out the garage.

One of the items he found was a peculiarly shaped brass pot. Doug thought: "What the hell, maybe it's a magic lamp. I'll give it a couple of rubs and see what happens." So he did and to his surprise nothing happened. He threw the pot into the trailer.

When he had a full load, he went to the dump. The pot was in one of the armfuls of trash Doug grabbed from the trailer. It fell to the ground as he made his way to the edge of the landfill. He didn't want to drop everything and try to pick it up so he started kicking it to its final resting place. On the fourth kick, a cloud of colored smoke came out of the pot and a genie materialized before him.

"Just a minute," said Doug. "I rubbed that pot three times and nothing happened. What's this all about, anyway?"

"Well," responded the Genie, "there's been a change in the rules. The union met last year and we decided to switch from three rubs to four kicks. You see, everybody and his brother caught on to the three rub routine. Every time anyone saw anything made out of brass, they'd give it three rubs and we'd have to come out.

"There was no place to hide. We were being called on right and left. We were being worked to death - and the wishes we had to fulfill! Do you realize bust measurements averaged 28 inches before all this magic got going?"

"Oh, I'm not interested in stuff like that," said Doug. "I'm too busy hunting and fishing and building ice shanties and tying flies and . . ."

"Not another outdoors type", groaned the genie. "Just my luck. I'm getting awfully sick of having to produce trophy specimens for you guys. Last year's world record black bear almost ruptured me."

"O.K, O.K," said Doug. "Just give me the standard three wish package - power, a million bucks, and a cabin on a trout stream."

"You're my kind of guy," said the genie who then got a funny look on his face and began to sweat and grunt and make dreadful noises. He got a little indistinct, slowly turned into colored smoke and disappeared back into the brass pot.

Doug didn't feel any different and began to think the whole episode was nothing but a figment of his imagination. When he went home to get another load of junk, the telephone rang. It was the Governor who announced Doug had been appointed to fill the unexpired term of a Senator who had just been executed at the federal prison.

So Doug packed up and went to Washington, D.C. It was not a happy time for him. Doug wouldn't take bribes, sell influence, cheat on his expense account, file phony election funding reports or take kick backs from his office staff. This was a terrible precedent and when the other members of Congress found out about it, Doug was ostracized. Some tried to have him impeached for conduct unbecoming of a Senator.

The folks back home liked Doug. He became popular. When he came up for reelection, they showed their esteem and appreciation by soundly defeating him. You see, political office is conferred upon people the voters don't like. They give the bum a job on the condition that he leave town and live in the capitol. A defeat at the polls is like a pardon.

Back at home, Doug was in more trouble. The Internal Revenue Service wanted to know where he got the $1,000,000 that had been deposited in his name in the local bank. A review of his previous income tax returns gave no hint of how he could accumulate that amount of money. They wanted to know where it came from.

When Doug came forward with the story about the genie, the IRS didn't hesitate for a moment. They charged him with perjury, trafficking in drugs, all unsolved bank robberies and defrauding the government. As a result of all this, the Democrat Party considered him qualified to run for Governor, but Doug declined the nomination.

When the dust had settled and Doug paid the fines levied by the judge and the unpaid state and federal income taxes, together with the interest and the penalties, he had just enough money left, after selling his homestead, to pay his attorney.

With his reputation ruined and his finances in shambles, Doug remembered his third wish, the cabin on the trout stream. He searched through the safe deposit box and, sure enough, there was the deed to property in an area known for its fine trout fishing. Having had enough of civilization, Doug grabbed his fly rod, jumped into the 4-wheel drive and headed for his fishing property. He left the highway and followed the two rutted road until he saw a new cabin appearing through the evergreens.

And he lived happily ever after?

Don't be ridiculous.

As advertised, the genie had given him a cabin on a good trout stream. That was the problem. It wasn't near a good trout stream, it was built on a good trout stream - right smack dab on top of it.

When Doug was unable to produce either a building permit or an Environmental Impact Study, the Department of Natural Recourses and the Environmental Protection Agency brought charges. Doug was forced to admit building in a flood plain and impeding the navigation of a stream. He was found guilty and sentenced to five years in Philadelphia, without time off for good behavior.

MORAL: Don't clean out your garage.

The Will of Carmichael

I, Carl Carmichael, being of reasonably sound mind and knowing that eternity is long and life is short, especially if I keep hanging around that bunch of Wolf River trout fishermen, do hereby make, publish and declare this to be my Last Will and Testament.

ARTICLE FIRST

Being of said sound mind, it is my intention to spend all of my money during my lifetime and be flat broke at the moment of my death, thereby cheating my doctor, my lawyer and the funeral director out of fat fees. However, it's possible I may not live out my allotted three score and ten years and, instead, meet an untimely end before I can use up all of my assets.

If there is anything left over when I go, I direct my Personal Representative to vigorously resist payment of any claims against my Estate. Did it ever occur to you that the reason these debts haven't been paid is because, during my lifetime, I considered them to be unjust, improper and/or outrageous? - like the debt I'm sure Jack Allord will try to collect.

Last November, I paid the farmer eight hundred dollars just because I shot his cow by mistake. Allord made me sign a note for the three hundred dollars I had to borrow in order to make the full payment.

Well, it was Allord who insisted we have a couple beers

before heading back to deer camp and it was Allord who stopped the car when we saw those big eyes shining at us from over what turned out to be the manure pile next to the barn. Any right thinking person would know Allord was more to blame than I.

O.K. Allord, put this in your pipe and smoke it. I purposely misspelled my name when I signed that note. I direct my Personal Representative not only to resist any attempt you may make to secure payment of the note, but also to visit the District Attorney and swear out a Complaint charging you with forgery.

ARTICLE SECOND

I direct my Personal Representative to lay my split bamboo fly rod, Hardy reel, all of my flies, my fly boxes and leaders, a good supply of #12 Mustad hooks, my Lefevre 20 ga. shotgun and a couple cases of 7 ½ chill shells next to me in the casket.

I realize this will make their burden much heavier so apologize to my pall bearers for me. Tell them why I made the request. Just in case I'm wrong and there is an after life, I want to be properly prepared.

ARTICLE THIRD

I'd better leave a thousand dollars to the Catch and Release Society of America. Reincarnation is a possibility and I may come back as a Brown Trout.

ARTICLE FOURTH

Paul Eckert has been a good and faithful friend of long

standing. We've hunted and fished and told lies together for a lot of years. Give him whatever .32 caliber cartridges are left in that cigar box in the bottom dresser drawer. They're kinda old and green but they'll still fire. Paul is one of the few deer slayers who still uses a .32 Special.

Come to think of it, Paul has been such a good buddy I should leave him more than half a box of old cartridges. Paul always wanted a new .308 but, what with the costs of college and a wife with access to a credit card, he's had to put the purchase of a deer rifle low on the family list of priorities. I know how badly he wants one. He told me he'd do absolutely anything to get one.

Since gold is selling for a pretty good price, knock out my teeth and give them to him. He can sell the gold fillings for enough to buy a good rifle. However, to be on the safe side, if I'm shot in the back and the Coroner digs out a .32 caliber slug, don't give him a damned thing.

ARTICLE FIFTH

In the national interest, I leave my graphite/boron fly rod to the youngest U S Senator representing my state of residence. I recommend all other trout fishermen make similar provisions in their wills.

Over time, the old Senators will die off and then all members of the Senate will have fishing rods. If we're lucky, they'll start trout fishing. If they do and we're very lucky, they'll become fanatics and spend all of their time fishing. Since the well-being of the United States is inversely proportional to the amount of time Senators spend in Washington D.C., we will save the country.

ARTICLE SIXTH

Dave Otto's major joy in life is chasing the canny Ruffed Grouse. He has never disclosed the location of his favorite hunting spot to me. I've never told him where my secret grouse covert is hidden. If I told him, I know he'd keep the information completely confidential. I certainly wouldn't divulge the location of my spot during my lifetime.

Though Dave is trustworthy, I'm not going to tell him where it is after my death, either. This one goes to the grave with me. Who says you can't take it with you?

ARTICLE SEVENTH

I was going to give my collection of duck and trout stamps to Rob Cowdery, but I've changed my mind. I just found out he kept putting slugs into my 12 ga. skeet gun when he challenged me to a clay pigeon shoot. That's the kind of low trick one would expect from a conniving, crafty counterfeit.

I admire and respect him for it and wish I had thought of it myself, but I didn't and he did and he won fifty dollars from me and that part hurts, so to hell with him.

On second thought, give him that five acres of swamp land I own up in Florence County and make sure he has to pay the accumulated back taxes. I took the property for a bad debt. It's worthless. He'll never be able to get rid of it. Put a big value on it, too. Then he'll have to pay an inheritance tax.

ARTICLE EIGHTH

The rest, residue and remainder of my Estate, real and personal, wherever located, I devise and bequeath to the

Internal Revenue Service. Sooner or later, they're going to get it anyway.

ARTICLE NINTH

I nominate and appoint the Governor as my Personal Representative and direct that no bond be required of him. I require no bond not because I trust him to manage my Estate without getting his hand in the till. It's because no insurance company would consider bonding him and I won't ask the impossible.

IN WITNESS WHEREOF, I have signed this Will this 20th day of September, 2011.

his

CARL   X   CARMICHAEL

mark

Silver Threads Among the Gold

When the class reunion is held and Mel Robertson, who nobody has seen for fifteen years, appears, he is apt to go unrecognized. There will be a lot of peering at his name card. By the end of the evening, his classmates will say: "Did you see Mel Robertson? Great Scott! He has turned gray and bald and fat."

The chances are his classmates, their husbands and/or their wives have also turned gray and bald and fat, but they haven't noticed it. Physical changes, we are told, are gradual. Aging is a slow process, like the oxbowing of a stream. Little by little and year by year the human being's wiring, tubing and muscles wear down and begin to disintegrate.

That may be so, but it isn't a complete explanation. There are a lot of exceptions. There are too many men who are old at age 40. They've lost their zip. They act like they're over the hill - and they are. They awoke one morning and decided they weren't young anymore. Thereafter, they were old.

On the other hand, we should be cautious about using only advanced age and gray hair as reasons to call a man "old". I believe most of our ideas about "old" hunters are inaccurate. I believe they are a result of chicanery and deception, perpetrated by some of the world's most experienced deceivers, impostors and liars.

Every camp contains at least one of those rogues. At 8:00 in the evening, the "old gentleman" says: "Gig, would you be so kind and bring me another scotch and water?" Gig looks at him, collapsed in the camp's most comfortable easy chair after tramping around in a cedar swamp looking for a horned whitetail. Of course, Gig answers: "Sure, Ed."

So Gig does it. It makes him feel noble. After all, the old timer may not be around for too many more seasons. Deer hunting must take a lot out of him. You have to admire him, at his age, out there hunting in the snow and cold. The least you can do is make him feel comfortable in camp.

Well, friends, if this has ever happened to you, and I know it has, you have been taken in by a consummate con artist. Go back over the day's events. Who was up until 3:00 a.m. playing poker? Who was out of bed at the crack of dawn complaining about the coffee? Who was the first in line for the bacon and eggs? Who was on only one drive? It was less than a quarter mile long and mostly down hill. And who got out of both washing and drying the dishes?

Who will sit up until the wee hours, getting scotch and water served to him and telling stories, and who will be up at the crack of dawn complaining about the coffee? Old Ed, that's who. If you think back, Old Ed has been getting his drinks brought to him and getting other preferential treatments for well over ten years. There's nothing fragile about Old Ed. He has the constitution of a rhinoceros. If you don't believe it, try this:

Sometime, when Old Ed is within ear shot, casually mention to one of your camp mates that Ed is getting kind of old and you're worried about his physical condition. Suggest that Ed shouldn't be invited to deer camp next year - for his own good, you know.

You'll see a startling metamorphosis. Come the next sunrise, Old Ed will prepare the breakfast and wash the dishes all by himself. He'll take a part in every drive and clean and haul two deer out of the woods without assistance. After he's split a cord of wood and washed the dinner dishes, he'll want to go into town and kick over a few fire hydrants. You wouldn't be able to get him out of deer camp with nitroglycerin.

Old Ed make have counted over sixty birthdays. He may have a wrinkle of twenty around his eyes, forehead, nose, ears, mouth and neck, but he can drive thirty feet of 1 ¾ inch well pipe in a day and wade through 300 yards of springtime white water in the Horse Race Rapids without missing a cast

The next time he pulls that wounded snipe act and asks you to bring him a drink, the proper response is: "Get it yourself, you damned old fraud. And while you're up, don't you think it's about time you brought me a beer?"

The reason Old Ed isn't old is because that thought has never occurred to him. So he's young - and more power to him. Disintegration is a terrible thing.

Last year, Beecher Daniels walked into Casey's Sport Shop to buy a hunting license. He was a rugged featured, slightly wind burned, well muscled, middle aged man. He entered the building as a youthful and perhaps even a jaunty man. He left the shop a stoop shouldered, shaky and trembling ancient - all because of the kid behind the counter.

Everything was going along just fine as he questioned Beecher and filled out his hunting license application. Then the little cretin came to the question "Color of Hair". The kid looked up at him, said "Gray" and dutifully inscribed it on the form. In a split second, he aged Beecher by twenty years.

From time to time, Beecher noticed some iron gray clipping on the sheet the barber wrapped around him. He had wondered where it came from, but no one ever told him he had gray hair. Now the kid told him he was an old man. Beecher managed to walk all three blocks back to his home without stopping to catch his breath. Then he looked into the mirror. By

George, the kid was right. His hair was turning gray.

Beecher called the undertaker and made arrangements for a Funeral Trust. He reviewed the terms of his Will. He pulled out the TV Guide and looked for the time of the Lawrence Welk Show. He was practicing his cackling when his wife came in. She told him how terrible it was that their neighbor would wear such a shockingly tiny bikini to get a sun tan in her back yard.

Beecher suddenly remembered how the roof needed repairing. He grabbed some shingles, a hammer and roofing nails. He climbed up on the railing, swung onto the roof and ran, leaping over the gables like a gazelle, to that part of his roof that overlooked the neighbor's back yard.

It occurred to him he wasn't so old after all.

Cocktail Parties

Hunters and fishers are required to endure larger annoyances and are exposed to greater miseries, agonies and distress than are the other less fortunate kinds of men. There's no justification for it, but there's no doubt about it, either.

Two theories have been advanced to explain that curious phenomenon. According to one hypothesis, those persons who do not participate in our field and stream activities, noting our particular serenity and joie de vivre, become uncontrollably jealous and dedicate their lives to bedeviling us. A listing of these kinds of persons include people in the IRS and the DNR and wives.

According to the other theory, the Architect of the Universe knew he was creating a favored class of superior people when he made sportsmen. He gave us additional burdens to carry in order to keep the others from crying discrimination and favoritism.

To test the second postulate, I recently ran a scientific survey. I questioned all of my hunting and fishing acquaintances. Without exception, every one of them agreed, unreservedly, that hunters and fishermen were all admirable fellows, endowed with a markedly superior intellect. I showed these decisive results to What's-Her-Name and she said: "Humnphf," thereby proving the first hypothesis.

The fact that additional sufferings have been assigned to the sportsman is incontrovertible. Consider the increases in license fees, the uncontrolled growth of recreational rafting on our trout streams and the probability that we will be dragged off to some wretched social event where we will be expected to wear a tie.

When the little woman has her heart set on going to the Koenigs for wine and cheese next Friday "because I hear Alyce has redone her bedroom and I want to see it and all of our friends will be there and you haven't taken me out since the opening of the trout season last spring" - well, take my advice friends, give up. Don't fight it.

Oh, I suppose you could come out with: "Aaeegghh, kakka kah hakk. I didn't want to worry you hon, but yesterday I went to see Doc Fischer for a check-up. He says I've got the Black Plague. It's very contagious. Maybe you'd better go without me."

It won't work. She's almost certain to remember Doc Fischer is a veterinarian. If she doesn't believe you, that tale will put an additional strain on your, at best, rather tenuous relationship. If she does buy it, you'll only be postponing the inevitable. You might as well get it over with. You know you'll have to attend one of those affairs every year or so. It's part of the special price you must pay for having the magnificent good fortune of being an outdoorsman.

All right then. You're at this party and you're bored to death. You haven't said a word in an hour - except for "Yes, dear" and "Ha, ha." Your hostess will think it is incumbent upon her to bring you into the mainstream of the party and make sure you have a good time. She has read the books on the hostessing business. She has learned to put a guest at ease by starting a conversation on some subject in which he is interested.

When she gets that look in her eye and advances toward you, be prepared. You're in for a question about the Great Out Of Doors.

A common question is: "Why does a doggie hold up one of his paws when he points at a birdie?" The answer is: "A hunting dog will frequently interrupt a step as it closes on a bird. Thus, a front foot or a hind foot, may be held in the air as the dog freezes and rigidly indicates the presence and location of a quarry. But be just a bit careful with the raised hind foot. I got fooled once."

Last year, Doug Burris was hostess engaged, as follows: "My husband is a duck hunter. What does he mean when he talks about six chilled shot?" Doug answered: "Drinking warm whiskey on a cold day is considered by some to be injurious to your health. Your husband, madam, is addicted to sitting in a duck blind and drinking whiskey after it has been chilled for six minutes."

When you're at a party, it's important to pay attention and not let your mind wander. Bob Gartzke got into trouble at a Bryn Mawr social event. He was thinking about ice fishing while his hostess was going on about bird watching. She claimed she saw something quite spectacular during the previous summer.

Bob regained consciousness in time to hear her ask if he could identify it. She said it had a yellow tail and caught flies. Bob said it must have been a Chinese outfielder.

Anyway, when Alyce Koenig approached, I was ready for her. She asked me: "How does one stop a dog from jumping up on one?" In a good loud voice I said: "Kick him square in the..."

At this point What's-Her-Name apparently had an attack of something. She let out a scream and became quite agitated. She grabbed me by the arm and hustled me out of the house. I got into the car and drove her straight home. She didn't say anything. She seemed kind of white and tense and she made gurgling noises.

In a few days she was back to normal. It made me feel good - taking care of that social obligation. A man really should take his wife to one of those parties every once in a while.

Improving the Breed

I count a number of dentists among my acquaintances. I wouldn't call them friends. I don't know anyone who calls a dentist a friend. While I wouldn't want my daughter to marry one, I can unequivocally say I carry no deep and abiding grudge against the members of that profession. Like most of you, I would meet with one of them - in the darkness of early morning and on a deserted road - to privately hunt or fish with him.

However, in case you haven't noticed, it is quite clear that dentists are just a wee bit "touched". While not, perhaps, serious psychic disorders, they display peculiar and aberrant behavior patterns. The tapestries of their character and personality contain more than one strange thread.

For Olympic quality "strange", the naming of Doc Pomeroy would be followed by a motion to close nominations and direct the Secretary to cast a unanimous ballot. The Doc enjoys the hunt. When grouse, woodcock, pheasant, duck or quail occur, he'll take out a shotgun and tramp the fields and coverts. All sober, lucid and normal, you say? Well, don't be too quick to jump to any conclusions, friend. Listen to this:

For a number of years, it was Doc Pomeroy's usual practice to spend Thursday evening attending a meeting of the Society for the Suppression of Saxophone Players. The stated aim of the Society was praiseworthy and attracted the participation of solid intelligent townsfolk.

At the weekly conclaves, the members presented thoughtful

papers covering such matters as the promotion of legislation to declare possession of a saxophone to be a felony and the amending of the Oath of Allegiance to require prospective citizens to swear they were not now and never had been a member of any organization dedicated to the playing of the saxophone.

The social hours following the business meetings were vigorous. Last December, after a particularly stormy session in which a lot of caustic remarks and personal comments were made about a member of the Society, the group voted 27 to 1 to disband and reconstitute themselves as the Society For The Suppression Of Curmudgeons Who Drink Scotch Whisky And Smoke German Cigars.

Doc Pomeroy simply couldn't understand how such a previously intelligent group could adopt such an unreasonable bias against those who promote fine traditions. In any event, he took his bottle of The Macallan and his box of German cigars from the Society's locker and resigned his membership. This left Doc's Thursday evenings open. He decided to embark on an in-depth study of dogs.

You may think this interest was engendered by years of bird hunting and a friendly involvement with and sincere affinity for our canine companions. You'd be wrong. The Doc had a long existing prejudice against anything that swam, flew or walked on four legs, including dogs. While useful in the hunt, dogs, otherwise, represented inconvenience and trouble.

Doc Pomeroy found his life style requirements were satisfied by limiting his canine association to hunting with people who had good dogs. The Doc owned a dog once. It couldn't hunt, but always let Doc know when a stranger approached the property. Whenever it sensed the presence of an intruder, the dog would shove its tail between its legs, crawl under the bed and cower. The dog ran away one spring. Doc considered advertising for it, but concluded it would have been a waste of money. The dog couldn't read.

Doc's newly found interest in dogs was understandable. The more he saw of mankind, particularly after the unpleasantness at the Society's December meeting, the less he appreciated the genus Homo sapiens and the more he respected animals.

Aided by his free time on Thursday evening, scotch whisky and German cigars, Doc began to wonder about the characteristics that would be found in a perfect dog. He came up with: A perfect dog is "trustworthy, loyal, helpful, friendly, courteous, kind, obedient, cheerful, thrifty, brave, clean and reverent." He should also have a good nose and like to hunt.

How great it would be, thought the Doc, if dogs (a) didn't have hides that smelled like rotting gunnysacks when they got wet, (b) had such pride in their body surface that they would remove burrs and ticks without human assistance, (c) had a smaller stomach to reduce the expense of the food needed to operate them, and, (d) would eliminate one of the most onerous of the tasks of dog ownership by burying their own by-product in a neat and sanitary manner.

After all of this heavy thinking, the Doc was sure he was capable of developing a program of cross-breeding that would develop the perfect bird dog. First, he borrowed Tim Nickash's Black Lab, Lothario. Next he decided to use his garage as the ... (I don't know what you call it. I mean I know what you call it, but I'm not sure they'll print those words. Let's just say...) the place of assignation.

Being a neophyte in the cross pollination business, Doc got right in the garage arena with the participants. He thought he might be able to introduce the parties and, perhaps, help them along.

Well, the Doc will get out of the hospital next week. The

transfusions helped take his name from the critical list, but it will be some time before all the stitches can be removed. He never should have tried to breed a Black Lab with his wife's Siamese cat.

Chapter Two

The Uplands

The Uplands

It's a nice time of year. Blue skies, white clouds and green grass can't help but compare favorably with the somber gray/black of January and February. So, in the spring, a young man's fancy, if he has had proper upbringing, lightly turns to thoughts of picking morel. Trouting is just around the corner and there is no doubt about it. Spring is a marvelous time of year.

However, a lot of people prefer the fall. The reds, browns and yellows of that season also have their partisans. The bow hunting season, honey mushrooms and the woodcock all contribute to autumn's attraction. I think one of the major reasons for the popularity of autumn is the Tetraonidae family, more particularly, the vexatious Bonasa Umbellus.

The uninitiated probably think I'm referring to a Godfather of some Sicilian Mafia family, but, of course, you know we are considering the Ruffed Grouse.

Vexatious? Absolutely. You can study its habits. You can cross-examine loggers and pour over government contour maps. You can bribe timber cruisers and game wardens to locate its territory. You can even spot coveys in late September and you still may not see a feather on opening day.

The Ruffed Grouse knows twenty-nine ways to make a fool of you. Moreover, it's learning new ones every year. It can reduce a first class trap shooter to tears. It can give a man good reason to consider the immediate execution of his $500 bird dog. Yet, I know of no one who has voluntarily given up grouse hunting. Every bird season seems to bring something special.

Remember the time you shot and watched the grouse sail out of sight without missing a wing beat? Remember, how there were lots of witnesses hovering about and how you were the subject of a barrage of insulting commentary? Remember how your dog then came out of the brush with the bird in its mouth?

(It happened to Mark Shropshire four years ago. His hunting companions will never forget it - possibly because Mark keeps reminding them.)

No rational person would ever eat a woodcock, but hunters shoot (at) woodcock. QUESTION: Why? Being rational, as all hunters are, they wouldn't think of cooking it. ANSWER: They don't want to disappoint the dog that, with straight tail and uplifted fore paw, is frozen on point saying: "Here it is, boss."

Only an unfeeling lout would let his dog spend all the effort needed to locate the bird, show its expertise by holding the bird in place until the hunter arrives and then rob the dog of its retrieve. The very least the man can do is shoot it to show the dog his heart is in the right place. If he misses, it's his responsibility to explain his failure to the dog.

The dog is an essential partner in autumn hunting. As a result, there are three kinds of upland hunters. There are hunters who have no dog. They are content to take walks in the woods, carrying a shotgun. There are hunters who have dogs, like to take walks in the woods with a shotgun and like to make the gun go "BANG" every once in a while. Finally, there are hunters who like to take walks in the woods, make the gun go "BANG" once in a while and have no dog.

There is a fundamental difference between Type 2 and Type 3 bird hunters. Type 3 people have wives who become unruly, hysterical and real hard to live with when they find dog hair on the living room furniture. Divorce is usually out of the question. Neither party wants to run the risk of having the judge order them to take custody of their children.

Type 3 sportsmen quickly learn how to resolve their dilemma. They hang around dog trainers, attend field trials and strike up acquaintances with all and sundry who own hunting dogs. They provide food and drink to the dog owners and get invited to hunt with them. The cost of the food and drink is less than the cost of maintaining a dog.

There's something else about autumn that is attractive to rational people. It's not only the beautiful colors. It's the harvest season. The berries - blue, elder and rasp - make their appearance. So do the nuts - hickory, hazel and political. Each year, more and more people become involved in gathering nature's woodland abundances. The popularity of the collecting of wild foods can be proven by the sharp increase in mushroom poisoning deaths occurring in September and October.

For the upland shooter, life begins with the Autumnal Equinox. It is the time when fishermen metamorphose. Shedding their outer covering of waders and creel, they pick up scatterguns and become bird hunters - that is, the ones that have good dogs (or the ones who have access to them) become bird hunters.

A few days in the October woods is all that is needed to explain why many outdoorsmen prefer the third season. To commemorate that time of year, here are six essays about dogs and mushrooms and grouse and woodcock and autumn.

Hunting Economics

"Don't put your trust in money.
Put your money in trust."

As you proceed down life's highway, if you keep your eyes open, you'll come in contact with some curious characters. As an example, no one can spend much time on this planet without meeting somebody who has an acute case of the frugals. It has been said there are people of the hunter/fisher persuasion who fall into that category.

It staggers the imagination to think that a fisherman would be penurious when it comes to essential expenditures like a boat, a motor or a graphite/boron fly rod. Likewise, a dedicated hunter would never be stingy when purchasing a shooting iron or hunting clothing. Nevertheless, we have all met folks who enjoy camping, hunting and fishing and are otherwise quite snug with the buck.

Freddie Sydney was an example. He never married. He thought it was a dreadful waste of money. He rented his autos, too. Freddie followed the advice of Polonius and was neither a borrower nor a lender. He claimed lending people money gave them amnesia and the thought of paying interest to anyone was a concept completely foreign to him.

Freddie Sydney was tighter than the bark on a paper birch tree. Nevertheless, he owned quality shotguns and rifles, his fishing gear was top shelf and he drank only the best of Kentucky bourbons. Freddie had two dogs with excellent reputations. They had good bloodlines, were well trained by professionals and represented a heavy investment. Freddie loved to shoot over them. Though he enjoyed the accumulation of liquid assets, he wouldn't think of parting with either animal, even at the inflated amounts he had been offered.

Freddie's income was not among the nation's top twenty percent, but his expense ratios were low and that was the secret of his comfortable economic status. A conservative investor, he was dividend and interest conscious, but he had the courage to sell and re-invest. Over the years, he built a nice portfolio of high income producing investments.

People believed Freddie kept a large amount of cash, neatly tied in easy-to-count bundles, stashed away in and around the leased ten acres that contained his home, a wood lot and a stream known to hold Brook trout. I always thought the story was a lot of hogwash. Freddie wouldn't keep cash when it could be producing eight percent or more in corporate preferred stock investments. The rumors, however, persisted and, I'm sure, were accepted as gospel by more than a few.

Two of those "more than a few" were Dean Massey and Carl Wussow. Massey and Wussow were the presidents of two local competing banks. Both of them would have given an eye tooth to get Freddie's reported hidden cache securely reposing in his depository. Whenever either of them talked to Freddie, soon or late, the conversation turned to representations of the absolute safety of their particular institution, the interest rate on term deposits and such stuff like that there.

Freddie never seemed to be caught up in the spirit of the thing. He never opened an account in either bank. He never borrowed a penny from Dean Massey or from Carl Wussow - both of whom considered such a situation to be the blackest of tragedies. It was a pleasant surprise, therefore, when Dean looked up one morning and saw Freddie standing in the bank lobby, nervous and ill at ease.

Dean's pulse quickened when Freddie walked into his office and sat down. Freddie wasn't carrying a little black box, but it was clear he was there for some special purpose. After an agonizing five minutes of small talk, Freddie finally got around to wondering what interest he might get on a bank deposit.

Dean began to salivate and figured the potential was so good he might give something above the usual rate. He said he'd pay 5 5/8 percent. He didn't know Carl Wussow had already quoted 5 3/4 percent.

Freddie went on for another five minutes of small talk while Dean managed to keep control of himself. Then Freddie wondered what the interest rate might be on a short term loan of two thousand dollars. Dean shaved the rate to 12 percent. It was a good move because a half hour earlier, Carl said his bank wanted 12 ½ percent.

Freddie supposed the bank would want a lot of collateral for a loan like that. Dean said absolutely no collateral would be required from a good, fine, upstanding, honorable and well respected citizen like Freddie Sydney. That was a mistake. The old conservative nature of Freddie's Scottish forbearers showed itself. Freddie said he didn't want any special treatment and he wasn't sure he wanted to deal with a bank that loaned money without taking collateral. The bank might go bust.

He got up to leave. Dean blocked Freddie's way to the door and hastened to assure him that the bank usually took security, almost always took security and, in fact, he couldn't remember a case in which the bank didn't take security. He would certainly be willing to take security from Freddie and why didn't Freddie sit down while they discussed the matter.

Freddie agreed and came straight to the point. He had a chance to take a fishing trip. The opportunity developed without notice and, unfortunately, his next dividend and interest installments would not be received for another two or three weeks. Freddie had the dismaying option of selling an investment, borrowing short term or missing the fishing trip. The least disagreeable alternative was to borrow the money.

The only security Freddie could give was his two dogs, worth well in excess of two thousand dollars. Dean was happy to lend Freddie the money. Freddie insisted Dean take the dogs hostage to secure the loan. The deal was struck. Freddie borrowed $2,000. He delivered the dogs and, after a tearful farewell, he left town.

Thirty days later, Freddie returned from a long fishing vacation in Alaska. He went to Carl Wussow's bank and withdrew the $2,000 he had put in a savings account just before he left on his trip. He also took the $9.58 of interest earned on his deposit. Then he went to Dean Massey's bank and gave him the $2,009.58 plus $10.42 of his own money. This paid for the $2,000 loan and the $20 interest charged for the month.

That wasn't so bad. Where else can you board two dogs for thirty days for $10.42?

How to Pick Mushrooms

My first two wives died from
eating poisonous mushrooms.
My third wife died from
falling down the stairs.
I couldn't get her
to eat the mushrooms.
- Joe Miller Joke Book
(1616 edition)

If you spend an appropriate amount of time stomping around in the wood, you're going to see fungi. They spring up like mushrooms. You'll see all those different shapes and sizes and colors and you'll become curious and want to learn about them.

Some of them, according to Mexican Indians and the long haired creep who lives down the street, are hallucinogenic. Some of them are not only edible, but delicious. Some of them will cure all of your problems, including that of continued breathing.

The ability of some mushrooms to promote an untimely (but, in your case, probably praiseworthy) journey to the bottomless pit makes the people who carve tombstones and the undertakers smile and rub the hands together in glee. There are other people, however, who view the presence of poisonous mushrooms with alarm.

Some of them recommend a detailed study of wild mushrooms before getting too enthusiastic about collecting, sautéing and then dumping them over your T-bone. Others waste no time on such sentimental rot. They believe any study of wild mushrooms can only result in an exacerbation of the world's serious overpopulation problem.

If you are one of the cowardly types, you'll probably want to learn something about picking mushrooms before actually engaging in the activity. A common way to learn about woodland fungi is from a book. Be warned, mushroom manuals will give you a quagmire of information and a series of convoluted classifications as intricate and as difficult to understand as the steps in an 18th century minuet.

Books that give clear and concise information on the matter of mushroom edibility are as rare as a liberal with common sense. Most of the literature on the subject is unenlightening and seems to purposely confuse and obfuscate. All you really want to know is: can you eat the damned thing or will it kill you. That's a simple question and it should elicit a simple answer.

O.K., let's see what the text books have to say.

1. The edibility of the Helvela Infula is described as: "Poisonous to some, but edible for most people." Aren't you glad you bought that book? Doesn't it make you feel warm all over? Now that you've been educated, how would you like to bite into a Helvela Infula?

2. The Amanita Citrina is characterized as: "Probably edible." In other words, if you eat one you will live - probably.

3. The Suillus Umbonatus is classified: "Edibility - nothing is known, but it is probably edible." If they don't know anything about it, how can they say it's probably edible? After all, the "probabilities" of being attacked by a giant Squid while walking down Walnut Street in Philadelphia are a million to one. Once is enough.

A lot of that kind of imprecise and confused scribbling appears in the textbooks. Is it any wonder the multitude cries out for a safe, sure and uncomplicated method for the picking of the mushroom? After considering the ignorance and superstition surrounding the world of the mushroom hunter, Tom Rosenow set out to create order from chaos.

Tom's experiment was not entirely successful. It produced equivocal results simply because some people are jealous and won't cooperate with those of us who try to advance the body of knowledge of the human being. I am convinced Tom's experiment would have produced a definitive answer to the fungi edibility question. It would have succeeded except for the uncooperative attitude of the people of Milwaukee.

Tom picked a large supply of a great variety of mushroom completely unknown to him. Then he sent samples to a hundred people whose names and addresses were taken at random from the Milwaukee telephone directory. He asked his subjects to eat the mushrooms and advise him of the results.

It was Tom's plan to publish a book which would show a picture of a fungus and, beneath it, print a terse and simple comment like: "This one is good to eat", or, "This one will make you throw up". I know you'll share Tom's disappointment in the way this scientific investigation of mushroom edibility was received.

He didn't get a single response. When he sent a follow-up letter, those Milwaukeeans proved their hostile antagonism by marking "Deceased" on the face of his letters and sending them back to him, unopened. The opportunity to have a book that would be truly helpful was, thus, lost.

There is yet another reason why you should be cautious about buying mushroom text books. I'm not too happy about the terminology they use. After all, from time to time there are children about the place. They have to be protected. The texts all contain words that are not nice, words that are quite suggestive and some words that are downright obscene.

To begin with, I hunt with Charlie Awen. Charlie is a M.D. Every once in a while we talk about medical things. I happen to know what the word "stool" means. When the mycologists write about "toadstool", I think they can be accused of bad taste, to say the very least.

Consider the fungus family known as Boletus. There's the Boletus Badius (but no Boletus Goodius). There's the Boletus Impolitus and the Boletus Luridus. This is the sort of thing that leads a fair minded person to conclude we'd all be better off if the mycologists would concentrate on determining which mushrooms can be safely eaten, rather than being preoccupied with the bad, the impolite and the lurid.

One kind of fungus is called "Stinkhorn". If you think that designation is deplorable, consider the Latin name they've hung on it. It's called Phallus Impudicus. I think the authors of mushroom books are all sex maniacs.

The Marasmius Oreades are commonly called "Fairy Rings" and the Clavaria Fusiformus are known as "Fairy Clubs". Hells Bells! I thought they were social organizations. When I got to the Lepista Nuda, I didn't read any further. I burned the wretched publication. I didn't want What's-Her-Name to find it and accuse me of going to the dirty book store, again.

If you are still interested in learning how to pick mushroom, you're in luck. I'm here to help you. I've picked wild mushrooms for nearly two years. In order to test them I've been slipping them into What's-Her-Name's soup and she's still alive. So, I qualify as an expert, and here, in print for the first time, is the Winter System for picking mushrooms.

1. Grasp the mushroom by its stem, close to its base, with the thumb and forefinger, exerting medium pressure. The arm should be parallel to the ground and bent at the elbow in about a 45 degree angle. The mushroom hunter should look directly at his thumb nail.

2. Keeping the thumb and forefinger in the same relative position, turn them with a clockwise motion (if right handed, counter clockwise, if left handed) using the arm as the axis. At the same time, bring the entire picking hand sharply toward the face for a distance of about four inches.

The result will be a picked mushroom. Practice using this technique. After a few weeks in the field, you'll be able to pick mushrooms with all the assurance of an expert.

To Hell with Dave Duffey

There's no doubt about it. Man is the hunting dog's best friend. Where would they be without us? We feed them and provide them with quality shelter. We take them for walks. We groom them. We keep their kennels neat. They are allowed to sleep on the living room furniture. We provide them with toilet bowls to quench their thirst. We send them to school and educate them. We take them on hunting trips. We even provide them with dogs of the opposite sex when the mood strikes them. You and I should have it so good.

And just how do they re-pay us? When we are alone with them, they'll heel, follow hand signals and retrieve. When anyone else is around it's an entirely different story. Their behavior patterns automatically reverse. They embarrass us.

We react by buying books on dog psychology and studying articles written by experts like Dave Duffey. For all I can see, none of it does a bit of good. For my part, I've had it up to here with articles dealing with bloodlines, protein content of puppy food, and such enlightening information as:

QUESTION: Should a dog be penalized if his handler uses a quirt, ostensibly to flush birds, but in a manner as to intimidate the dog?

ANSWER: If the handler deliberately intimidates it, the dog should be penalized.

Just what kind of academic nonsense is that? I've hunted with a dog named Chipper, and I use the term "hunted" in a very loose connotation. After an hour in the field, Chipper had me worked into such a state I was looking for a 2 x 4, not a quirt, to intimidate the little son-of-a-(deleted).

There were plenty of birds. Chipper worked one and a half gun ranges out. He flushed everything at that distance. He never came closer. I think he knew what would happen to him if he ever got within shotgun range.

Another dog, a German shorthair named Hans, did exactly what he wanted to do, not what you wanted him to do. If you ever tried to intimidate him or even raised your voice, let alone your quirt, Hans would snarl and look at you with yellow, malevolent eyes, so evil they would have scared the living bayjaysus out of Ivan the Terrible.

Now then, writers of hunting dog essays, why not tell us how to intimidate dogs like Chipper and Hans. That's the sort of information we real dog owner want. Forget about telling us how to treat sarcoptic mange. Give us something we can use.

While I'm at it, dog writers, you might just as well know that we owners of authentic hunting dogs are not too enthusiastic about your coverage of field trial where (I suspect) bionic dogs follow their owners' whistle signals, hand retrieve on command and perform other acts never seen in the real world. No dog I've ever owned acted that way.

We'd much rather read about everyday, plain working dogs - like Kingman Loomis' hunting mutt, Ginger. King calls her a kind of setter and pointer - an upsetter and a disappointer.

It was a real disappointment when none of you dog writers attended the field trials in Langlade County. The trials were organized by hunters and were meant to show off the characteristics of real hunting dogs. Our canine friends were judged in a comparison with dogs like Chipper and Hans and

Ginger, not those effete, pusillanimous eastern kennel pups.

The dogs were judged on their behaviors and abilities in Nose, Ear, Stamina and Retrieving categories. The first event was the Nose Competitions. The dogs were turned loose and retrieved 30 minutes later. Some had encountered skunk and one had rolled around in a very ripe deer carcass. The winner was the one who found a dead fish. The test area was nine miles from water. While the skunk finders were more odiferous, the judges felt the fish finder smelled rotten enough and its ingenuity in finding the fish deserved special consideration.

The second test was the Ear Event. The award for this competition went to an English Setter. In one half hour Tober collected 18 cockleburrs, 23 weed seeds, 7 woodticks and 2 blackberry bush twigs - in one ear alone!

The Stamina Event followed. The dogs were placed in the center of a cleared forty. The first one to cover the distance from hunter/handler to the tree line got ten points. Any dog staying within shotgun range was immediately disqualified. Additional points were given to the dogs who were lost for the longest period of time.

Yellow Lab named Buck took the Duck Retriever Cup. He returned to the blind with seven decoy lines hopelessly entangled in his legs. His nearest rival could claim only five.

The major award went to Boots, and American Water Spaniel. It was a popular choice. The assembled multitude was impressed by the dog's cowardice and patent fear of water. His enterprise in shaking cold water down his owner's neck, unexpectedly and from unusual distances, together with his ability to shiver and look miserable put the animal in contention. After Boots crept out of the blind and got onto the rug before the fire in the cabin without the judge or owner noticing, he was a shoo-in for Worst of Show.

Take heed, dog writers. These are the sorts of subjects you should explore. Owners of hunting dogs can relate to them, but I suppose you'll all go right on producing articles about dogs that point and heel and obey their owners and look respectable.

Dave Duffey, go soak your head.

Vile Bodies

If you have a 50/50 chance
of shooting a woodcock,
nine times out of ten,
you'll miss.
- Old Indian Proverb

One of What's-Her-Name's cats caught a chipmunk last summer. He deposited it on the back steps, sat next to it with a pleased expression on his face and waited for the accolades of an appreciative mistress. The cat got chewed out for (A) disturbing the ecological balance of the neighborhood, and (B), bringing the corpse home. The cat sniffed, looked superior, turned and slowly walked away.

A few years ago, Tom Trowbridge came out of the woods with a handful of woodcock. He brought them home, deposited them in the sink and, with a pleased expression on his face, waited for the accolades of an appreciative mate. Barbara took one look at them and said: "You know you don't like woodcock. You know I don't like woodcock. Why do you bring them home?"

Impressed by the logic of her question as well as by her firm tone of voice and arched eyebrow, Tom thought it would be a good idea if he gave them to a friend. "Not on your life," rejoined his mate. "Do you want to ruin a nice relationship?" So Tom arranged to have them delivered to an enemy who didn't know much about woodcock. Tom not only got rid of them, but also had the added satisfaction of imagining the scene when his victim tasted the cooked bird.

The cat's system is a more direct and efficient method for

disposing of vile bodies. Dropping them and walking away has much to say for it, but the system is ill-suited for those of us who prefer to avoid having our wives throw dead woodcock at our retreating heads.

The Trowbridge Method is more complex, but has an advantage. It serves the secondary purpose of getting back at some numbskull who has incurred our ire. It cannot, however, be recommended as a regular strategy for divesting oneself of dead timber doodle because hunters are usually admirable fellows and, as a consequence, we have few enemies (if you don't count police, gun control nuts, owners of posted land, wives and the Department of Natural Recourses).

Now, I know there are people who think the problem of disposing of dead woodcock is not one of the major crises facing the Republic. I know they base this mistaken belief on the fact that woodcock are hard to hit and few of them, thus, require disposal.

True, there are more ways of missing a woodcock than there are ways of missing any other game bird. Many, many more ways of missing them. From time to time, however, you will bust one. You might try to eat the first one you bring home, but if you have the IQ of a rutabaga, you'll never try to eat a second one. Then you'll learn just how hard it is to get rid of unwanted woodcock.

It's not an easy task, lads, but great challenges have always engaged the imaginations of great men and great solutions are usually forthcoming. How else can you explain the inventions of smokeless gun powder, hip flasks and brassieres that open from the front?

John Tincher was one of those rare and gifted men. He hunted woodcock. His dog retrieved them and he took them home. Moreover, on occasion, he could be prevailed upon to take some of the ones his companions shot. During all the time

I knew him, John was always a gentleman and never, never tried to palm one off on me. This made me wonder what he did with them.

John never talked about a recipe for woodcock and he never mentioned actually eating one. I respected him too much to suspect he might be engaging in such an unspeakable practice. To be on the safe side, however, I never accepted an invitation to dine at his home for fear that Isabel might have cooked one for dinner.

All hunters must be prepared for the time when they are trapped into attending a meal where woodcock are served. The Winter Salvation Program is recommended by many serious students of the subject.

The Winter Salvation Program consists of taking a few spoonfuls of wild rice, or asparagus, or something other than the woodcock, then choking, then remembering you are allergic to whatever you just tasted and announcing you must stop eating immediately or you'll break out in large purple and orange splotches.

To my relief, I found out John Tincher was not eating woodcock. He had developed a unique and profitable system for unburdening himself of the unwanted birds. He had kept it secret for over twenty years. After I solemnly promised never to use his device or describe it to anyone, he took me down a deserted road, again swore me to silence and then explained it to me.

Here it is. John would go out of his way to become friendly with every sporting goods store operator in the area. He would bribe them to give him the names of anyone who bought a Smoker. Some of those who bought the smokers would not be bird hunters. John would nuzzle up to them, bring up the subject of smoking game and effect surprise when the victim admitted his recent purchase of a smoker.

John's scam consisted of mentioning how lots of folks thought woodcock breasts, when properly smoked, were one of the finest of the world's gourmet delicacies. John would say he was allergic to smoked fowl, that he had enough woodcock for his own simple needs and would be happy to provide the victim with an ample supply of the breasts in exchange for smoked salmon or venison.

John got a good supply of smoked meat and was able to get rid of two and, sometimes, three batches of woodcock before the victim discovered there was no way, smoked or otherwise, to make them acceptable to the civilized palate.

Skepticism

In spite of the Federal Truth in Advertising laws, guaranteed, you will recall, to protect us all from falsehood, some people suspect statements made by advertisers are calculated to mislead and deceive us. Even the promises of politicians, made as they eagerly shove and push their way toward the public payroll, are often accepted with a grain of salt. The truth of pronouncements coming from government agencies are, in some quarters, subject to serious doubt.

Yes, friends, we live in a time of suspicion and disbelief - a time when the magazines at the check-out counter sometimes don't tell the actual truth - a time when even the accounts reported by fishermen are questioned. I, for one, think it's just terrible. Just Imagine! People going around not believing other people. Whatever is happening to our standards? It's gotten so bad you can't accept as absolute gospel the statements appearing in black and white in sportsmen's publications.

An outdoor sports writer, who claimed to be an expert on the bird, reported the average Ruffed Grouse had 18 to 20 square tipped tail feathers and an overall feather count of between 4,300 and 4,500, not including down. To the average citizen, this is great information. It can be used to amaze his friends, win drinks down at the corner saloon and elicit yawns from his wife.

To the doubter, however, something quite different is apt to happen. Carl Skoog was not a grouse hunter. He was one of those suspicious and skeptical types. Carl had trouble believing liberal politicians and network newspersons. His doubting nature was aroused by the "4,300 to 4,500 feather, not including down" report.

"Hmpf," he said to himself. "The author of that pamphlet makes his living by writing. He doesn't have time to sit down and count the number of feathers on a bird. If the author's wife has brains enough to qualify as an imbecile, he wouldn't be able to con her into doing the counting, either."

It occurred to Carl that the writer's wife could have agreed to do the counting. She could have taken the bird, disappeared into a room and, a few minutes later, come out, declaring: "There are exactly 4,375 feathers on that bird, not including down." No one who can count to fifteen without removing a shoe would believe she actually counted them.

Carl was skeptical. He asked himself: "Just what does that guy mean when he says 'average'? It suggested that someone counted the feathers (not including down) on more than one bird. "Hogwash," Carl thought. "Nature faking," he scoffed. "By George," he again said to himself, "It's about time that fraud was exposed."

Carl applied for a federal grant to study Ruffed Grouse feathers and was given $100,000 by the Department of Interior, on the condition he somehow come to the conclusion that Gun Control was necessary for the well-being of society. With the hundred thou, Carl bought a flame orange hat, a pair of light Chippewas, good brush pants, some chamois shirts, a 12 ga. over/under, improved cylinder/open choked Beretta, shooting glasses, two cases of 7½ chilled shotgun shells, a trained grouse dog (with bell), a 4-wheel drive vehicle and a case of single malt scotch.

Now reasonably equipped, Carl began to wander around the northern part of the state in search of the Bonasa Umbellus. Being an urban type, Carl's first season was not an unqualified success. A portion of the grant funds were spent paying fines for shooting Rhode Island Red chickens and for hunting without a small game license. The 4-wheel drive vehicle was abandoned to a deep woods sinkhole and had to be replaced.

When both cases of shells had been fired without producing a single specimen, the season was coming to a close. Carl found a shifty eyed, crooked looking, dirty local who agreed to sell him a pair of grouse. The shifty eyed, crooked looking, dirty local turned out to be an off-duty game warden. He wasn't even wearing a disguise. Carl was sentenced to six months in the county jail.

As you all know from your own personal experience, when you spend six months in the county jail, friendships are formed and a certain camaraderie develops among the incarcerated. Anyway, while spending the winter in the county hotel, Carl met a number of accomplished grouse hunters. They are known to regularly nest in the jail during the off-season.

By the time he finished serving his sentence, Carl's newly found grouse hunting friends included disbarred attorneys, defalcated bankers, a few dentists and a doctor who had been convicted of under-charging, which is strictly forbidden by statute.

With part of the remaining grant monies, Carl bought another case of shells and three cases of single malt scotch drinking whisky. He spent the next fall hunting with his new buddies, searching for the illusive birds. His second year was a success. Carl shot two Ruffed Grouse.

Carl's wife, Delores, did New York Times crossword puzzles and always came in out of the rain. The suggestion that she count the feathers, not including the down, resulted in hysterical laughter. So Carl started picking and counting, all by himself. It required careful use of tweezers and extreme concentration. Carl was up to it.

He started at the bird's head and, after ten hours, had counted over 3,500 feathers, not including down. He could see the end of his task. It was really too bad Delores asked him if he could remember Jim Herman's telephone number. If he hadn't broken his concentration and answered, perhaps he would have remembered where he was in the count.

The system for the count of the second bird consisted of putting the feathers, not including the down, in neat, easy to count, 100 unit piles. After appropriately chastising her, Carl enjoined Delores from talking. She sat by, silent and subdued.

Personally, I believe Carl's count on the second bird would have been accurate if Delores hadn't become curious, looked over Carl's shoulder, got a feather in her nose and sneezed.

The jury found Carl Not Guilty by reason of temporary insanity.

The Rites of Autumn

During the first half of October, whether or not the moon is full, an uncommon and irregular group of Ruffed Grouse shooter-aters and their dogs give their guardians the slip and convene in the wilds of Wood County. The dogs do not have guardians although their association with that particular group of hunters gives rise to serious question about the levels of their intelligence. No one has ever inquired into the IQs of the hunters. No one has had the courage to plumb those murky depths. The hunters' sanity, however, is recognized by everyone as being borderline at best. How else can their annual visit to Wood County be explained?

The forays into the green shard in search of our feathered upland friends are carefully planned out months in advance. Timetables are established. Maps are reviewed. Patterns for sequential movement over adjacent hunting turfs are meticulously plotted. All of their planning is disregarded as soon as they reach the camp site. Getting those hunters into any semblance of order is as difficult as trying to organize a cub scout meeting, a government bureau and a flock of teal, simultaneously.

One competent dog will be in attendance. He'll work well and put up three birds. When the hunters fire and miss all of them, the dog will effect a look of disdain, stop hunting and spend the rest of the time exploring. He will answer no whistle, hand or voice signals unless it happens to be convenient and he was planning to go in that direction. His camp time will be spent under the truck in an attempt to avoid being seen in the company of the hunters.

A puppy is always present in camp. Its ability to hunt is nonexistent. Its owner has trained it to spill drinks, snatch anything vaguely edible from the unwary and cold nose the unsuspecting. Its owner is experienced in saying: "It's only a puppy". He can say it in nine languages. Unless that pup shapes up, it will not live to become a dog. If it continues to indiscriminately sample everything that comes out of the camp kitchen, death from ptomaine poisoning is assured

This brings up the camp food. I use the term in its regurgitative connotation. The biscuits and gravy were remarkable. The gravy is now being used in a Wisconsin Rapids Kindergarten as library paste. The biscuits serve as decoy anchors on Boulder Lake. The coffee had to be downed while still hot. When it cooled, it hardened in the mug and could not be removed.

And the exotic cookery! Preserve me, dear Lord, from another go at snake pickerel covered with defrosted wild mushrooms and seasoned with garlic powder and ginger. Experts have concluded the only way to safely dispose of the camp's garbage would be to encase it in cement and bury it deeply in solid granite, along with other primary atomic waste.

The camp honcho carries the honorific title of Director of Field Operations. The honor compares favorably to being tarred, feathered and run out of town on a rail. The DFO is selected in an entirely democratic manner. The one who draws the short straw has to serve. Perhaps he is a respected member of the community. Upon becoming the DFO, he is immediately transformed into a man as popular as Barack Obama at a Republican Convention.

He may be a judge, never overruled by the Supreme Court and before whom hardened criminals cringe in terror, but as

DFO he can't make a simple decision without facing a chorus of objection, complaint and insubordination. This crowd of rabble, themselves untouchables, treat the DFO as a pariah.

The poor man can do nothing but sulk and make empty threats while his hunting companions stare at him and await his next hunting decision which will evoke the questioning of his ancestry and intellect, hoots of derision and automatic disobedience. The anarchists could learn from this group.

The company is, indeed, a mixed bag. The townsfolk refer to them as The Four Horsemen of the Apocalypse - Famine, Pestilence, Death and Destruction. They have also been likened unto Sacco, Vanzetti, "Devil Anse" Hatfield and Billy the Kid. When the sun finishes coloring the sky and has retired below the horizon, the camp fire is blazing and the time for quiet reflection has arrived. Then all hell breaks loose.

The Director of Field Operations is given a terrible, verbal keel hauling. Billy the Kid viciously kicks at and misses the pup, which has gotten into the caviar. Devil Anse starts telling the Fred Schmidt story. In the middle of it, Sacco, Vanzetti and the Kid all get up and walk away. Devil Anse (the DFO) is pleased because, in their absence, no one is criticizing him.

Large parts of the remainder of the evening are spent cruelly exposing the inadequate hunting ability displayed by each hunter during the day- and they are legion. Sacco, who was last year's DFO, gets revenge by playing a tape recording entitled "Eleven Centuries of Classical Chinese Music". Ultimately, the pup eats the tape. He's not such a bad hound after all.

Vanzetti insists on reciting verse from The Shooting of Dan McGrew, Xanadu and Gunga Din. There's no place to hide. The DFO breaks out some of his home made wine. (It cured my hiccups.)

As far as the booze consumption is concerned, the entire

crew could serve as poster boys for the Women's Christian Temperance Union. Over the years, many times on Sunday mornings, I've heard each one of them proclaim he'd never take another drink as long as he lived - ever.

The Wood County excursion leaves the participants in a state of acute physical exhaustion. Each has been the target of unspeakable abuse. All this for a handful of Ruffed Grouse. I wouldn't miss it for the world. It's one of the Rites of Autumn.

Chapter Three

The Lakes and the Streams

The Lakes and the Streams

Alcoholic beverages are widely accused of turning the American brain into silly putty and being the major reason the mad houses are filled to overflowing. I wouldn't get into a fist fight with any of the ladies or gentlemen who hold that opinion, but I'm not convinced John Barleycorn is the true culprit. There are at least two pieces of incontrovertible evidence to the contrary.

First, it has long been well established that a dram or two of scotch whisky and an ice cube will remove the objectionable taste from water and, thus, has to be good for you. Second, consider the number of madmen abroad in the land. I don't mean merely those who attend rock concerts, criminals, feminnazis, economists, liberals, and newspaper editorial writers. I mean the public, generally.

Can you explain the television networks' selections of their programming without presuming they have firmly and unanimously adopted the concept that the viewing public has clouded perception? If you think Madison Avenue has a respectable opinion of the public's sanity, take another look at the commercials they create and send your way.

Here's something else to consider. How many people live in cities? Can anyone free from serious psychic disorder put up with city life? Next, review the quality of our elected officials. Could any sane person vote for them? Still, many of them get over fifty percent of the vote (excepting, of course, successful Chicago politicians).

Now then, after you have estimated the percentage of the population which is screwball, doesn't it become obvious that there isn't enough alcoholic beverage in the entire universe to occasion all that madness?

After a moment's thought, the true cause stands revealed. It's the water, friends, plain everyday water that has given people the crazies. About 95% of the human body is water. Three-quarters of the earth's surface is covered with it. Only a commodity that common and voluminous could account for the pervasive lunacy inhabiting the earth.

If you're still not convinced, consider the duck hunter. All of his activity is centered around water and he is known to do many very strange things. Would anyone with even a limited grip on reality come home at four in the morning and announce to his wife that he bought a live buffalo at the D U banquet for only nine hundred dollars?

After substantial government grants, university statisticians studied duck hunting and concluded: The better the ducks are flying, the smaller the percentage of the kill. It's true, even though it, like duck hunting itself, doesn't make sense. If a single duck flies past the blind of two hunters, it is clearly on a suicide mission. If four or five buzz the set, some of them have an excellent opportunity to escape with their tail feathers. Still, the action of those ducks can only be described as reckless and without regard of life.

However, if a whole flock of a dozen or more come at the hunters, their risk is minimal. Gun barrels will wave around like the flags of World War I navy signalmen. Weapons will be fired as quickly as fingers can react. When the smoke has cleared, nary a feather will float down to the surface of the lake. The only things the hunters will get is a reproachful look from their Labrador Retriever.

You want more evidence that people who associate with

water are a bit loose in the flue? All right. Some people study foreign languages like Spanish or German or New Yorkese. Duck hunters study duck. They spend hours listening to records and tapes which endlessly repeat the single word: Quack. If the people who listen to punk rock should be institutionalized, what can we say about people who spend so much time trying to earn to speak the limited language of a duck? It is loony, but such erratic behavior is easy to explain. Duck hunters spend a lot of time on the water.

Duck hunters are not the only ones affected by water induced silliness. Since everybody knows they are deranged, who but a mad man (i.e. a lake fisherman) would row a boat within range of a blind known to contain duck hunters - armed with shotguns - and proceed to fish for perch?

Stream fishermen are also on the waiting list for rooms at Bedlam. They spend hours working at a tiny vice with some feathers, some string and some fur. Then they'll take the product of their labors - a hook with some stuff tied to it - and say to a companion: "Look at this grasshopper." It looks as much like a real grasshopper as Zasu Pitts looks like Marilyn Monroe. This is the same kind of manic delusion which allows the certifiably demented to proclaim: "I'm Napoleon."

It's the water that does it. The lakes and the streams and the rivers are responsible for a lot of madness. If you want more proof, here's half a dozen examples.

How to Pluck Ducks

A man doesn't know
true happiness
until he gets married.
Then it's too late.
-Socrates

Back in the good old days, life was simple. A man didn't have to spend most of his time chasing the almighty dollar. Game and fish were plentiful. There was no Women's Lib, punk rock or income taxes. Steel shot had not been invented and it was a good time to be alive. I'm referring to the Stone Age, of course. Mankind's serious problems began when it ended. I know exactly when that momentous event occurred. It happened like this:

The Pterodactyl hunting season had opened and a cave man was returning from a successful day in the field. He had clubbed his limit (723 points) and, as usual, had one helluva time dragging the birds from the swamp, through the tar pits and up the hill to his cave. When he finally got there, sweating and out of breath, for the first time in history, a wife said: "You killed them. You clean them".

That was it. An era had ended. Since that time it's been one damned thing after another and mankind has had to face a nearly endless list of disasters - including Attila the Hun, the Black Plague and the Obama Administration.

Oh, it hasn't been all agony and despair. It can be argued that civilization has progressed in some ways. Consider, if you will, the advances made in the development of the double barreled shotgun and in the distillation of single malt scotch drinking whisky.

Personally, I'm optimistic about the future of the race and believe we will solve the vexing problems that confront us. Surely, a collective intelligence that can send a man to the moon can figure out a way to get wives to pluck ducks.

Ever since that cave lady's revolting comment, we've been able to get them to act only after coming up with a satisfactory answer to the question: What's in it for me? Back in the good old days, there was an easy response: "Hon, if you don't have those Pterodactyl plucked by the time I get back from the corner saloon, I'm going to pick up a stone ax and pound the hell out of you. Bye, sweetie. I'll see you in a couple of hours".

Some thousands of years later, an alternative system was developed. It went like this: "Christmas is coming and, if you're as good girl, I'm thinking about doing something very nice for you."

Up until the 1920s, it is chronicled that the system worked well. Then, everything went to pot. Prohibition, women's suffrage and auction bridge held the country in their scaly grasp. The Charleston and the speakeasy produced the flapper. Neither offers of bribery not threats of intense pain were sufficient. "How'd you like a punch in the nose", or "Would you like some jelly beans" just weren't enough to motivate the 1920s female into a duck plucking mood. New and imaginative methods were needed. They were forthcoming.

The Togetherness Approach and the Pectoral Movement scenarios evolved. For nearly half a century, wives plucked millions of ducks through their usage, but they weren't always successful. The Togetherness Approach failed Pete Scheinert. He tried it. Daisy didn't buy it. It went like this:

Pete: "Gee, hon, I feel a little bit selfish about my duck hunting."

Daisy: "Just what do you mean?" (She sounded a bit testy. There was an indication of suspicion, but she's been fooled a few times and isn't as credulous as she used to be.)

Pete: "Well, I get all the enjoyment. I get to shoot them. I get to clean them. I get to cook them. You don't seem to have any of the fun."

Daisy: "Humnmphf." (She didn't rise to the bait, so after a while, he tried again.)

Pete: "The Ladies Home Journal has an interesting article. Togetherness. Mmmmmmmm. You know, a husband and a wife really ought to do things together. Taking hunting, for instance. I wouldn't want you to sit in a freezing duck blind and I don't think it's right for me to ask you to cook them." (He certainly wouldn't ask her to cook them. Her wild game cooking has caused more stomach disorder than the Spanish Flu. The Department of Health offered him $5,000 a year if he would keep her out of her own kitchen.)

Daisy: "You mean you're going to give up duck hunting and spend those fall week-ends with me?" (There seemed to be panic in her voice.)

Pete: "Well, not exactly. I thought we could have a lot of fun if we would take the feathers off the birds - together."

Daisy: "The last time we did anything together was when we beat up the minister who married us. If I have any more togetherness with you, I'll scream. You shoot 'em. You clean 'em."

If the Togetherness Approach fails, try the Pectoral Movement Scenario. The PMS has produced favorable results for a number of my associates. It consists of convincing your soul mate that plucking ducks is just great for bust development. In my own case, What's-Her-Name's response was: "Listen, Mr. Wonderful, I'm wearing D cups now. If there's any more development, I'll get stoop shoulders. Besides, didn't you tell me mowing the lawn would do the same thing?"

It is safe to conclude you won't be able to expect results from the PMS unless you are fortunate enough to have a small busted wife.

In any event, now we are in the 21st century and things have changed. Women have the vote and are wearing tight slacks. They subscribe to our sport magazines and they study our outdoor supply catalogs. They look a lot better, but they are harder to fool. A new ploy is needed. In the interest of keeping one jump ahead of them, I offer a system that has been called: Winter's Sure Fire. Here it is.

Select a catalog that advertises 100% goose down jackets. Bring it home some evening and prepare for action. Start slowly.

You: "Gee, Hon, will you look at this jacket ad. They want $289.95 for it."

She: "$298.95! Humnmpf. I hope you don't think we can afford that." (This is definitely not a question.)

You: "I'm afraid you're right, Hon. But I really did want to buy one for you."

She: "Oh? For me? Well. Oh."

You: "You've got the bod for it, Hon. I don't believe any of your girl friends have one. They're really very warm and light."

She: "Let me see that ad. How much did you say they were? What colors do they come in?"

You: "Too bad they cost so much. Saaaaay, I've got an idea. . ."

Got the picture? You buy a pattern for a jacket and she starts plucking ducks and saving the down. Every February, you sneak into the basement and steal a couple handfuls of feathers from her bag. Depending on how poor a shot you are and the size of your hands, it can take her ten years before she has enough down to make a jacket. By that time, she may have become accustomed to plucking ducks and you'll have it made.

Honesty is the Worst Policy

The fisherman has established a pretty good reputation with the rest of mankind. He isn't associated with violence. He is pictured as calm and contemplative, a pipe smoker, kind to his mother and little children, friendly and pleasant to be with - if you don't mind the smell of whisky and dead fish.

However, any member of the fishing fraternity who is completely unbiased, painful as it may be, will be forced to admit that we are not (all of us) perfect. True, fishermen are universally recognized as noble and wonderful. But to be fair about it, one modest criticism has been leveled at us.

We are reported to have a slight tendency to be selective in reporting facts. We are believed to have a predilection to the abstracting of unnecessary elements from our stories. We are said to suffer an intemperate and congenital need to add colorful emphasis to out representations. Putting it another way, people think we lie a lot.

Research into the history of fishing seems to confirm it. People have seldom believed us. In ancient Greece, when Diogenes lit his lamp and began looking for an honest man, he stayed away from the ports and waterfronts. Jonah, after a prolonged absence from home, returned to his village and explained that he had been swallowed by a large fish. The story is in the Bible and nobody seems to question it.

When I came home from a fishing expedition - only a few days late - and gave What's-Her-Name the same explanation, she didn't come close to believing me. It's enough to sour a

71

man on religion. Perhaps, I should have made up some lie and told it to her, but I find it very difficult to tell a falsehood.

Oh, I don't mean fishermen should be such paragons of virtue that they must always, always, tell the complete, unvarnished and absolute truth. No one but a lunatic would expect you to do other than commit perjury in response to the question: "Where did you catch that four pound Brown trout?" You'll still go to Heaven if you say it was at the Chipmunk Rapids on the Wolf River when it really at the bottom of the Porcupine Rapids on the Pine.

The doors of the state prison will not open and swallow you up if you report using a Pas Lake fly when, in reality, it was a Muddler Minnow that did the trick. As a matter of fact, there is good reason for those modest deceptions. The truth would have resulted in herds of people trampling the vegetation on the banks, splashing around, muddying the water and disturbing the delicate ecological balance of the beautiful stretch of the Pine River that contains one of your own favorite fishing holes. You may have saved the stream from destruction.

A proper description of the fly you used would start a run on the market, raising the cost of the Muddler Minnows and adding fuel to the terrible inflationary trends. It would also result in unemployment of Pas Lake fly tiers. Any fool can see society should praise fishermen for exercising a bit of guile. It protects both the economy and the environment.

Moreover, telling the pure unadulterated truth will, almost certainly, get you in trouble. It can be dangerous to your health. Clevis Dewlap dislocated his shoulder and had to go to the hospital when he tried to show Dan Diminico the size of the Northern that got away on Shawano Lake.

Disclosing only the truth would clog up the court system. Think of the number of divorces that would be started if truthful answers were given to such questions as: How much did you spend for that fly rod? - or - You're not planning on once more spending our entire vacation fishing, are you?

If you think honesty is the best policy, consider the (unlikely) possibility of politicians telling the truth. What would happen? They wouldn't get re-elected, that's what would happen. Then they'd return from the capitol and live back here with us. As unemployable, unskilled laborers, they'd all be on welfare. Think of how your property values would go down if they moved in next door to you. We should be happy they are all liars and have been deported to Washington, D.C.

Comparatively speaking, fishermen are models of honesty Nevertheless, throughout the entire civilized world, people think the fisherman treats the truth in a cavalier fashion. He is unceremoniously lumped in with such consummate deceivers and dissemblers and used car salesmen, liberals and defense lawyers. It's the same in the uncivilized world, too.

Somehow it doesn't seem right. A person will plan his life, or, at least, his weekend on the basis of the 10:00 o'clock report of some TV weather man who hasn't told the truth since the summer of 1982 - and then it was by mistake. But if you say: "I was canoeing up on the Gunflint and I had my spinning rod with me...", that same person will effect a look of patent incredulity and rudely punctuate your remarks with crude expletives. It's enough to set one's mind adrift.

The situation is so bad, I am very reluctant to report fishermen's factual case histories. Like the time Jim Habeck was bass fishing with Tom Grover. There were some big bass around, but nothing in their tackle boxes would attract them. Tom said bass would sometimes go for a frog and, about that time, Jim heard a splash. He saw a snapping turtle in the lily pads about two feet away from the boat. It had a frog in its mouth. Jim grabbed the turtle before it could swallow the frog, but he couldn't get it out of the clamped jaws.

Jim wasn't interested in getting too close to the snapping turtle's mouth because they can bite your finger off at the elbow. He took out his hip flask and poured some scotch whisky down the turtle's throat. Then he did it again. Sure enough, in a little while the turtle started humming. When it opened its mouth to sing, Jim retrieved the frog and threw the turtle back in the water.

Jim hooked up the frog and cast with it a few times. Then he heard another splash. The turtle, quite purposefully, was swimming back to the boat. It had another frog in its mouth.

Quack, Quack, Quack

Duck hunters and other people of genuinely superior intellect are inquisitive by nature. All surveys concerning members of the water fowling fraternity show the rest of the population considers them to be curious types. You will often see duck hunters wandering around wondering about some serious problem. You can tell they are in deep thought by the pained and dazed look on their faces, like they've been out in the sun too long.

Go to any D.U. Banquet and you'll find them apparently paying no attention to what is going on about them. They are, in all probability, thinking about some momentous problem - like the Incredible Olive Quandary.

Why do the holes in pitted olives always enter from the end and never from the side? What kind of specialized machinery can do such delicate work? Or, is it done by hand? Are there factories in Spain filled with dark eyed beauties, seated in production lines, patiently cutting the ends from olives and sucking the pits therefrom?

Further down the production line, after the posts occupied by the Pimento Stuffers and the Pimento Snippers, are there others with long thin fore and middle fingers who poke the olives into those long skinny bottles and make sure the pimento side always faces outwards?

Duck hunters worry about things like that. They also worry about the Great Duck Call Enigma. While some of the better minds of the country have been trying to find out why allegedly rational member of society will sit in a duck boat during a November snowstorm, very little attention has been paid to important matters like balancing the budget or reducing unemployment or solving the GDCE.

The GDCE is, indeed, a puzzler. For every Duck Stamp issued in the state, two duck calls are sold. This ratio between Duck Stamps and duck calls has remained stable for as long as records have been kept. Now then, duck calls are not biodegradable in the usual sense. They do not easily rot, nor do they disintegrate. If dropped in water, they float and can be retrieved.

People do not use wooden duck calls to start fires. You cannot find used ones in Flea Markets. Second hand duck calls are not advertised in the Shopper's Guide or on E-bay. Duck hunters usually own one, sometimes two, but almost never three of them.

QUERY: If the supply need not be annually renewed and, on average, a bit more than two are sold to each hunter every year, why are we not, all of us, up to our navels in duck calls? What happens to used duck calls? There is little serious writing on the subject. No article on the phenomenon of the disappearing duck calls can be found in the scientific journals. Clearly, the academic community or the government should commission studies.

The theories explaining what happens to duck calls should be collected and published. If we would stop frogging around with investigations of how the universe started and pay attention to the GDCE, maybe we'd begin to see some significant progress in the advancement of the human condition.

Some private studies of the matter have been undertaken. While results are still fragmentary, a few hypotheses have been developed. Two of them are noteworthy. The first is called The

Wallinger Response. This theory has been named after George Wallinger in order to give him proper recognition as the inventor and prime promulgator of the famous "Go Away" call which is popular with so many duck hunters.

Accounts of reliable witnesses establish that with just one of his clarion blasts, George has been able to clear a seven mile lake of all waterfowl, including coot. Chickens from neighboring farms have joined in the resulting migration.

The Wallinger Response suggests a partial explanation for the disappearance of duck calls. Other duck hunters will row across a lake, approach the blind containing the Wallinger response duck caller and, shotgun in hand, tersely call out: "All right. You with the duck call. Give it here. Now."

Not all duck calling, I hasten to add, does violence to the ear. Yes, there are those who's use of the duck call produces only raucous, blatant and irritating sounds, but there can be a melodic quality to proper quacking that approaches the beauty of a Giuseppe Verdi aria.

For example, it has long been my practice, late on the summer evenings when I am unable to sleep, to sit on my back porch and practice the mallard "Come Back" call. It is a wondrous sound. I regularly have the satisfaction of seeing the lights turn on in my neighbors' bedrooms, watching their windows raise and hearing them, red of face, shout out encouragement to me.

Since I am blowing calls at the time, I cannot hear exactly what they are yelling and, thus, am unable to give you a word for word recital of their compliments. Suffice it to say I know they enjoy the episodes by the friendly way they shake their fists at me. They've even called the police so the officers, too, can enjoy the dulcet duck call tones. Surprisingly enough, during daylight hours my neighbors seem to avoid me.

The GDCE is of particular interest to me because I have to

buy six or seven calls each year. They all mysteriously disappear. I don't know what happens to them. It's peculiar.

While digging in the shrubbery last spring, I found two of them. When I mentioned the discovery to What's-Her-Name, she turned pinkish, babbled some and developed the ET Theory. She suggested a group of Extra Terrestrials may have stolen my duck calls and inadvertently dropped them while scurrying back to their flying saucers.

This seems like a plausible explanation. In late August, fishing with grasshoppers and cricket dry flies is productive. I tie a lot of them and carry a good supply in the sheep skin on my hat band. It's always nice to have a few extra terrestrials with you.

September Song

Trout fishing on the opening day in mid-May is largely a ritualistic affair. The water is too high and too cold and too muddy and there are too many damned fools crowded into your favorite section of the stream.

Last year, Don Doherty found fishermen throwing streamers into a run of fast water he usually had all to himself. He walked past them saying to himself: "There are too many damned fools crowding into my favorite section of this stream." Silently, he contemplated the world's over- population problem. As he passed by the fishermen, Don heard one of them mutter there were too many damned fools crowding into his favorite section of the stream.

The first day of the trout season is a chilling ordeal. The temperature of early spring trout water is only part of the reason. The other part is the fact that trout fishermen wait until the opening day before they test their waders for leaks. They test their waders for leaks by wading, rib cage high, into trout streams.

Except for those who practice in the winter by running over greased bowling balls, after a seven month hiatus from wading in the fast spring-time river currents, the chances of filling one's waders on opening day is estimated at seventy-eight percent. Early spring fishing is hard to justify. Certainly, it proves, beyond a reasonable doubt, that people who are kept off trout streams for more than half a year become punchy and not responsible for their actions.

When late September occurs and the Ruffed Grouse and woodcock season has arrived, most folks have had their fill of searching the rivers and streams for trout. QUESTION: Is there a lucid explanation for fishing on that final day of the season?

Of the number of trout fishermen still out of jail when late September rolls around, a half dozen men, with enough gear to provision an African safari, meet on the banks of the Wolf River. They squeeze into two eight man rafts and float to their favorite trout hangouts.They disembark, unlimber their fly rods and proceed to beat the water into a frothy foam.

The Wolf harbors Brown trout as big as your leg. They rule the deeper pools above and below the many rapids. Occasionally, they rise to eat a kayak or send some fisherman into a state of shock. Unfortunately, these Browns are also smart. Fish experts claim they have an IQ in excess of 42. This makes them twice as smart as the average trout fisherman and much too quick witted to be seriously considered for public office.

The six worthies who spend the last day of the season on the Wolf justify their actions by claiming they are giving those humongous Browns one more chance to bust a line before the Department of Natural Recourses calls time and fish and fisherman bid each other their autumnal adieux. Each year this same bunch meets at a cabin near the river. They have a trout feed. The next morning, they begin to execute a previously concocted plan. It is such a masterpiece of disorganization it would make the angels weep.

The alarm clock is wound and set for an hour and a half before sunrise. This gives them time to dress, prepare breakfast, haul their already laden rafts to the launching point, paddle to the Oxbow and start fishing as the sun rises. In the morning no one pays any attention to the alarm clock - possibly because no one got more than two hours of sleep - possibly because a number of them insisted on telling stories all night long - possibly because single malt scotch whisky is said to have the power to loosen men's tongues.

Soon or late, the rafts are in the water. They hopscotch each other at the rapids. Raft #1 fishes the first and third rapids. Raft #2 fishes the second and fourth. The island below the Little Cedar Rapids, the fifth one, is planned as the site of the camp kitchen and the luncheon rendezvous time is set at 12:30.

The first raft to arrive at the island carries the grill, the charcoal and the wine. The coals are glowing by 12:30. The raft carrying the steaks, the caviar and the cheeses arrives an hour and a half late. They find cold ashes in the fire pit. They are unable to find any wine. Somehow or other, it has disappeared.

It was the responsibility of Wayne Pashke to procure the wine. While browsing in a Green Bay beverage shop, he found some stuff identified as a Rumanian Cabernet Sauvignon. The price was right, so he bought a case. It is easier to tell a book by its cover than to tell the quality of a wine by its label.

Pashke's wine wasn't exported from Rumania. It was deported from Rumania. The CIA thought it was part of a Communist plot to destroy our way of life. It required no little sacrifice on the part of the occupants of the first raft to protect the other fishermen by drinking all of it before they got to the island. And they had to drink it. If they poured it in the river it would have killed all the downstream fish.

The following spring, Wayne used some of it to clean the mold that had accumulated on the old leather chair in his cabin. It worked better than any commercial cleansing agents. He gave another bottle to the neighborhood alcoholic. He took one swig and gave up drinking. Another bottle was used to marinate an oak board. Wayne said it didn't taste good, but it was soft and pliable.

While the occupants of the second raft vainly tried to build a fire with wet driftwood and green alder branches, the inmates of the first raft descended upon the cheese and caviar like locusts descending upon Ethiopia. Of course, the steaks were never eaten at streamside. The fishermen in the second raft were hungry and short tempered. The fishermen in the first raft were not quite as hungry and in a much better mood. Insults were exchanged. Waders were filled.

The expedition was a disaster. It gave a new and deeper meaning to the word "anguish". Nobody except, perhaps, the certified occupants of an asylum would voluntarily return for a second such outing. Still, those six otherwise sensible people will, year after year, not only meet every fall to partake in this end of season lunacy, but will also actually claim they enjoy it.

The word "trout" comes from the ancient Greek word "tructa" which means: "nibbler". This suggests the old Athenians were worm fisherman and, thus, explains the reason for the decline and fall of the Greek empire. As yet, no one is sure of the etymology of the word "fishing". When the experts have finished their investigations and come to a conclusion, I'll give you two to one odds the word "fishing" and the word "insanity" will be shown to have a common root.

Fish Story

I've known Ollie Hitch for years. He's been hanging around trout streams for the major part of his adult life and is what you might call a "purist". He used only dry flies. He only fishes up stream.

Ollie has an unreasonable fear of bear. He carries a small .38 special under his waders. I don't think he could hit anything with it, but Ollie figures if he is ever confronted by a bear on a trout stream, he'll make the gun go "BANG" a few times, scare the living hell out of the animal and give himself the opportunity to get some space between him and it.

Besides suffering from bearophobia, Ollie has a few other peculiarities. For one thing, he suspects the DNR actually knows what it is doing. For another, he fishes with those tiny size 28 flies and he ties them himself. In my youth, I fooled around with those itty bitty hooks. My eyes were better then and I could tie them to the necessarily whispy one pound leaders after only twenty or thirty tries.

Back in those days, I, too, firmly believed the axiom: "The smaller the fly, the larger the trout", but that was last year and I'm smarter now. It occurred to me that if that axiom were correct, then the reverse concept would also have to be true: "The larger the fly, the smaller the trout" - and that is ridiculous.

I've fished the Madison in Montana with a nymph, locally known as a Bitch Creek. (I sure hope the typesetter doesn't make a mistake and spell it "nympho". If he does, this time

What's-Her-Name will leave me for sure. Things have been a bit strained around the house since the publication of the How To Pluck Ducks story.)

The Bitch Creek is about five inches long and has to weigh at least three pounds. It catches great, huge Browns and Rainbows. I know a big fly catches big trout. I simply don't believe a big size #2 Mustad hook can catch a small two inch trout. Any fingerling with the brains of a garden slug will be frightened of large artificial flies and give them a wide berth.

As a result of all that heavy thinking and the progressing loss of my 20/20, I seldom use size 28 flies. I still tie them, but only for a limited purpose. Occasionally, the mosquitoes and the no-see-ums get pretty bad. Then I use one of my own itty bitty flies, being careful to match the hatch. Any insect, flying around my head, will notice the quality of my hand tied fly, mistake it for a real one and try to mate with it. My back cast will usually break their necks. After a few false cast, I've cleared the air of the pesky insects and can again use normal sized wets, dries or streamers.

From time to time, Ollie and I get into discussion of the "little fly/big fly" question. We argue about the degree of danger posed by black bear and debate whether or not he should be committed. I have to admit Ollie has a vivid imagination and uses it in his defense.

Ollie fishes the Tomorrow River and he likes to talk about it. He claims he was busily wading upstream a few years ago, throwing one of those teeny tiny fly imitations, when it was attacked and captured by a Brook trout. Ollie estimates the trout was less than two inches long, thereby proving my theorem: "The smaller the fly, the smaller the trout."

Well, Ollie went to horsing in his little Speckled trout and as he pulled it past the rock with the white spots on it, a nineteen inch Brown grabbed it, thereby proving Ollie's theorem: "The smaller the fly, the larger the trout". The Brown headed for the nearest deep hole, and Ollie headed for cardiac arrest. He had a three pound trout on a one pound leader.

Ollie fought the Brown for some time, keeping the pressure on the line to under one pound. He sweated profusely and prayed to all know deities. The Brown finally gave up and Ollie began to carefully bring it toward his net. About this time there was a whooshing sound and Ollie looked up to see a hawk taking a pass at his trout. The hawk missed the fish and Ollie knew it would wheel around and take another swing at his trophy.

Ollie reached into his waders, pulled out the .38 and let go at the hawk. The explosion convinced the hawk he didn't really want the fish. Ollie missed him and he flew away, but the shot killed a four point buck that had stuck its head out of the upstream brush to see what all the commotion was about. In all of the confusion, Ollie let his line go slack and the big Brown spit out the two inch Brook and got away.

If you are a jaded skeptic, I suppose you may not believe that story. The game warden didn't. Neither did the judge. He gave Ollie large fines for the undersized trout and the out-of-season deer. Still, you've got to give Ollie credit for imagination.

The Lion Will Lie Down with the Lamb
(But which one will get up?)

If you've been frittering away your time in Ruffed Grouse coverts, on trout streams, chasing the wily buck or trying to outsmart a big mouthed bass, you cannot expect to have your name engraved upon the stone that identifies the people who have received and merited world-wide recognition.

Yes, unless you change your shameless ways, when the history of the world is written, you will not be included among those who have left an indelible mark on human society - names like Adolf Hitler, Jack the Ripper, Attila the Hun and Vlad the Impaler.

Sportsmen! You stand accused of having an escapist mentality - of not assuming the responsibilities you owe to mankind. Think about it. There are a myriad of serious problems that beset and bedevil the earth. Terrorism and chaos are rampant. The Four Horsemen of the Apocalypse are thundering down upon us all - and just what do you plan to do about it?

If I know you, you don't plan to do anything about it, you bum. The world is coming to an end and you're sitting there wondering if 6 chill or 4 chill is best for Mallards. Shame, I say, shame on you. Where is your social conscience?

I suppose I shouldn't be too hard on you. Until last week, I, too, had adopted the attitude: I didn't cause any of these problems. I can't solve any of them. I just live here. But now I've seen the light. Between the end of deer season and the beginning of trout season, if it doesn't interfere with my fly tying, re-loading or ice fishing, you will find me in the forefront, opposing evil things, speaking out in favor of nice things, caring and, in general, feeling guilty and trying my best to make you feel guilty, too. It's what the socially sensitive want me to do.

It all started last Sunday. The weather was miserable, wet and uniformly rotten. It wasn't a fit day for man or liberal. So, instead of gamboling about in the field and stream, I was reduced to house confinement. What's-Her-Name had gone to church to continue to pray for my soul and I was in a brown study. The newspaper was lying on my lap and I was staring, transfixed, into the telly.

I regained consciousness in time to hear some TV newsman questioning some self-styled expert about what they perceived to be some kind of impending disaster. You should have heard the questions. You should have heard the answers. If those answers are representative of the intellect of our "experts" (and I believe it is) then we are all in trouble. We are surrounded by Neanderthals.

Hunters and fishermen spend a lot of time trying to outwit grouse and bass and trout, all of which have IQs slightly higher than the experts interviewed by TV anchor persons. Our hunting and fishing endeavors succeed about once in every ten attempts. The so-called experts' attempts to solve international problems, at best, have a success rate of one in 100.

Since the brains power of the above-mentioned animals is about equal to that of the so-called experts and since hunters and fishermen have a success ratio ten times as great as that of the said experts, it stands to reason that we would be ten times better able at solving the world's problems. After due consideration, I decided it was time for someone to settle the problems existing between the Palestinians and the Israelis.

I called Jim Olson, a Trout Unlimited activist and asked him, straight out, what he would do about the West Bank situation. At first he wasn't too helpful. He got all emotional and went on for a time about high interest rates and unreasonable security requirements. He thought I was inquiring about the West Bank & Trust Company.

I explained I meant the Arabs and Israeli's inability to get along together on the West Bank of the Jordan River. It only took fifteen minutes and he had a program guaranteed to bring lasting peace to the area. It was immediately forwarded it to the State Department. So far, the government has not contacted us. In the interests of getting them to move a little faster, we have decided to go public and disclose Olson's plan for peace in the mid-East.

First, wing dams and stone ledges will be build along the shores of the Jordan in order to get the water to move faster and lower its temperature. Next, the banks will be seeded and half logs will be stuck into the shore line at appropriate places. The half logs will provide sanctuaries for small trout and the seeding will create habitat for insects, thus discouraging soil erosion and providing for healthy year 'round hatches to feed fish.

Brown trout will be planted. The State Department will be asked to fund the formation of a United Nations corps of game wardens to patrol the Jordan River and enforce catch and release regulations. To insure interest on the part of local politicians, additional bureaucracies can be established to monitor water flow, study trout population growth, etc., etc.

The PLO will be given a franchise to establish a fly tying cottage industry and the CARE people will be asked to provide the locals, on both sides, with serviceable fly rods. Within five years, Arab, Israeli and PLO trout fishermen will be wading up and down the Jordan River. None of them are going to stand for rifle fire, exploding bombs or other loud noises spooking the fish.

Peace and tranquility will prevail.

Chapter Four

The Woods

The Woods

In a July, 1984 edition, the Los Angeles Times reported the history of a terrible problem on a 740 acre state park known as Angel Island. Hunting had been outlawed and the deer had no natural enemies there. As is the natural result of such so-called management practices, the deer population exploded. There wasn't nearly enough food for the increasing number of deer and they were all in danger of starvation. So the state shot fifty deer before they had to abandon the project. As is usually the case, a public outcry defeated common sense.

Subsequently, the California legislature proposed the introduction of coyotes on the island in the expectation they'd kill off some of the herd. I suppose they thought it was a more humane way of solving the problem than by hunting - especially since the fawns would probably be the ones the coyotes would eat. The lawmakers' suggestion was not adopted. It was feared the coyotes would frighten the picnickers.

In a magnificent display of ecological ignorance, the state and the SPCA then combined to spend $88,000 to relocate 200 deer. Apparently, California's abusive relocation of the Nisei during World War II gave its citizens a taste for such nonsense. About 85 percent of the relocated deer died before the end of the year.

Then a $30,000 private fund was established. Its purpose was to solve the deer over-population problem by providing birth control programs for the animals. At the time, I thought they were moving in the right general direction, but hadn't yet quite got the hang of it. If the birth control devices were distributed to the people in Southern California, the deer would have a better chance of surviving. After all, it's people who ruin wildlife habitat with their smog, their roads and their housing developments. Reduce the number of people and wildlife will prosper.

Well, California has long been recognized as the nut center of the universe. The actions of its legislature only prove we are living in a democracy where all folks are equal. The law givers of that state are just as stupid as the law givers in most of the other ones. Wisconsin may be a little different. In that state, the politicians' standard nightmare (i.e. failure to be re-elected) makes them more afraid of deer hunters than they are of nuts. Of course, that is because Wisconsin contains more deer hunters than nuts (a condition which apparently does not exist in California).

As a result, the Wisconsin Department of Natural Resources seems to be exercising better judgment in managing the deer population. There are more deer in Wisconsin now than there have ever been in its history. The Department places a heavy burden on the hunters when it asks them to keep the herd down to a manageable size. Hunters are barely able to meet their quotas.

The herd maintains excellent health, keeps increasing in size and extends its territory every year. The day may come when there are deer hunter's camps in Milwaukee County. It is my earnest hope I never live to see it happen. I think deer camps should only be built in the woods. I get nervous whenever I'm not at least 50 miles away from a fast food restaurant. A deer camp within sight of brick buildings is unthinkable.

Unless ignorance and superstition take over and the DNR

people abandon their successful program, vigorous deer herds will continue to survive in the state. I hope the smell and flavor of the deep woods deer camp will also survive, but the next generation may never experience it - the sizzle of water dripping from wool socks onto a hot 55 gallon drum wood stove - the mice in the kitchen area - playing poker beneath a Coleman lantern that doesn't quite give enough light to allow you to watch the dealer with all the attention you suspect he deserves - the charms of a wood pile (split your own wood and it will warm you twice). This is the stuff deer camps and deer hunting should be made of.

If you hang around the Legion Hall, you'll see some old army veterans. They may have survived the Battle of the Bulge or the invasion of Iwo Jima. They are remarkable for it. In another ten or twenty years, old deer hunters will be similarly honored for having survived deer camp cooking. Many a triumph, but many, many more disasters, will be recorded in the histories of camp kitchens. Camp cooks, too, are part of the game.

So are the stories. A few of them accurately report what happened in camp. More of them report what might have happened there. Still more of them report what a fanciful man imagined might have happened there.

Somehow it doesn't seem possible for a deer camp in Milwaukee County to produce that kind of hunting atmosphere regardless of the number of bucks migrating that far south. One important element, the wild woods, is missing. To many hunters, the words "woods" and "deer camp", if not synonyms, are very close relatives. That's why the following glimpses of camp life are entitled "The Woods".

How to Roast a Suckling Pig

Unless you are about to be shot by an irate husband, the day is approaching when you will become short of wind, weak of eye and no longer able to run through the woods and over the hills like the proverbial goosed moose. You may then become annoyed to discover your presence in deer camp is less and less essential to your younger companions and of diminishing joy to yourself.

Face it, Charley. It's in the cards. Nobody wants you when you're old and gray - unless, of course, you're a good camp cook. You can be grossly flatulent, bad-tempered, a convicted child molester or even a liberal, but you will, nevertheless, be welcomed into deer camp if you can cook.

Some of us have managed to grow old disgracefully, telling outrageous stories, behaving in a generally felonious manner and chasing deer, duck, wild turkey, old crow, famous grouse, girls, partridge, trout and woodcock and, at the same time, retaining the muscle tone and vitality of a forty year old. We're sought after wherever men meet to hunt, fish or tell lies, but we represent a minuscule portion of the hunting and fishing fraternity. If I were you, I'd learn to cook.

You could buy a cookbook, I suppose. It would probably be written by some skinny woman who has never been outside of New York City and wouldn't know a Honey Mushroom if it knocked her down and sat on her. She'd fraudulently pass herself off as someone who can tell you how to roast a ringbill. Or, you could hang around northern Wisconsin and listen to practicing camp chefs and bull cooks.

Steve Johnson has been cooking in camp for over ten years and he hasn't lost a man. If you're interested in developing a cooking ability that will assure you of a place in camp when you're ancient and wretched, try this on your old wood stove. It's Steve's recipe for Roast Suckling Pig.

Get a pig. It should not be younger than four nor older than six weeks. It should dress out at about twelve pounds. Kill it. Bleed it. Then put it in cold water. That will tenderize it. When it has cooled off, drop it in scalding water Now, pay attention. If you drop it in boiling water, you'll cook the skin and make it harder than hell to get the hair off. Follow directions.

Drop it in scalding water and slosh it around until practically all the hair has fallen off. Then take it out and clean it. Start at the tail with your pig hair scraper and work toward the snout, removing all the remaining hair. Wipe the carcass with a damp rag. Try to find a clean one.

Hang the pig up by its hind legs and gut it, taking out the eyes and tongue. Wash the cavity with water containing a little soda and then rinse it out with plain water. Wrap the carcass in a cloth. It will keep the flies and bugs off. Then hang it in a cool place and don't roast it until 24 hours have passed. If you've done a proper job, the pig is now ready for seasoning and roasting.

(If you are one of those people who don't happen to have a pig hair scraper handy, you can ask your butcher to supply you with a 12 or 13 pound pig with innards, eyes, tongue and hair removed.)

After you've rubbed the carcass and the cavity with salt, pepper and whatever other condiment you enjoy, you can take your pig and stuff it. Steve likes a simple bread stuffing - bread, clarified butter, milk, salt, pepper, water, sage, chopped onion, wild mushroom, bits of apple, orange slices, walnuts, pieces of fried sausage, parsley, thyme and diced celery. But, do something complicated if you prefer.

Put about two inches of this stuff on the bottom of a roasting pan and criss-cross a couple of wooden spoons or strips of kindling wood on top of it. It will help you remove the pig from the pan after it has been roasted. Stuff the rest of the dressing inside the pig, but don't pack it too tightly. If you do you may end up with a burst roast suckling pig on your hands or, more accurately, on the inside walls of your oven. Then sew up the cavity.

To prepare the pig for the pan, break the legs at the joints and tie them in a kneeling position.

Years ago, my uncle Emil worked up around Pearson as a timber cruiser. Uncle Emil has been accused of telling the truth from time to time. There are some people who claim they can prove it. He told me this story and I think it might be the truth.

It was during the mid-1920s. Things were a bit more primitive then and, with no undertaker in the immediate vicinity, when someone turned up his toes in the summertime, they planted him in a hurry. In the winter, when everything was frozen, they would put him in the wood shed until spring when both he and the ground thawed out, but it was summer and it was a particularly hot summer.

Some old settler gave up the ghost in the backwoods of Langlade County. The word of his passing was sent out. Friends and relatives would be arriving by horse and buggy throughout the evening and the following morning. A half barrel of beer, bread and sausages were set up in the Grange Hall for the convenience of the incoming bereaved. A casket was ordered from the local carpenter.

Now, this local carpenter was also the village drunk. When ordering anything from him, it was the usual practice to negotiate the total price, go with him to the lumber yard to buy the wood, nails and hardware and then pay him the balance when the job was finished.

Unfortunately, the usual practice was not followed in this case. The body was carefully measured and the exact amount - the exact amount - of lumber needed to build the coffin was calculated. Believe me, back in those days, carpenters didn't waste any lumber. The materials were bought and the mistake was made. The carpenter was immediately paid for the whole job. In cash.

Of course, the first thing he did was get hold of two Mason jars full of white lightning. He proceeded to nibble at them during the casket construction process. He built it and he delivered it to the Grange Hall, albeit two hours late. When they went to put the body inside the coffin, they discovered it had been built 4 inches too wide and about 8 inches too short.

This really wasn't so bad. The boys heaved the body into the box and made it fit by crossing the legs. You know, they made an X out of the parts below the knees. This made the body eight inches shorter. Ice was poured on top - to keep the corpse from maturing in the August heat - and, shortly thereafter, the funeral party began to convene.

Things went well for the first few hours. The keg was tapped, friends arrived, lies were told about the exceptional character of the deceased and the bread and sausage disappeared. In the midst of taking the collection for the purchase of another keg, a peculiar sound came from the coffin. Silence occurred abruptly and everyone turned in time to see the deceased poke his head out of the casket.

The Grange Hall cleared in seconds.

Some say the decedent came back to join the party, but that isn't what happened. The ice cooled the body and the muscles in the legs tightened, straightening them out. When that happened the head was forced to pop out over the top of the coffin. This is why you break the pig's legs at the joints and tie them together. You wouldn't want them straightening out during the cooking, and forcing part of the pig out of the pan.

Put aluminum foil around the tail and ears, otherwise they will over-cook and fall off, thus destroying the esthetics of the presentation of the roasted suckling pig. This, as Steve says, would be gahdam gauche. Roll up a ball of foil, push it inside the pig's mouth and shove the whole shebang into the oven.

Before you close the oven door, take the cover off the pan. I never told you to put the cover on the pan.

The oven should be pre-heated to about 350 degrees Fahrenheit. That's about 176 2/3 degrees Celsius. (I put that in to impress you.) If the speedometer on your wood stove is working, you should have no trouble keeping the temperature between 350 and 400 degrees for the 4-5 hours of cooking time.

You'll have to baste the pig every fifteen minutes. Use beer, Pepsi Cola or water until there's enough juice in the bottom of the pan. Don't baste it during the last thirty minutes of the roasting. Cook until done. How do you know when it's done? After four hours, puncture the pig's skin deeply. If the juice come out reddish, its got more time to go. If just hot fat spurts out, you're in business.

When you think its about a half hour before being done, take the foil out of the mouth and replace it with an apple. Put cherries in the eyes. Serve with a green vegetable and a beverage. A not-so-dry California Cabernet Sauvignon is good enough for deer camp.

If you are new at the camp cook game, there's one more step to take. Boil a bunch of hot dogs for your crew. You'll probably screw up the roasting of the pig.

Trouble

Lem Wright is a wise man. He manages to get more than the share of hunting, fishing and cabin time regularly allotted to man. He knows where the watercress grows and where the mushrooms are abundant. He likes animals. He talks to them. He doesn't care a bit if they don't answer him.

Lem has attained the serenity that comes with wisdom and understanding and evinces the development of a solid philosophy of life. If some top heavy girl throws her arms around him, fogging his glasses and crushing the cigars in his breast pocket, Lem won't get upset with her. He can take such trouble and adversity without flinching.

Lem told me: "I don't care what a man plans to do or how he plans to do it. He can always manage to get into trouble." Ain't it the truth. It was Lem's opinion that trouble is substantially more sinister than merely the logical result of a series of events you, yourself, have put in motion. Oh sure, if you put up a shop to distribute pro-miscegenation literature right next door to the headquarters of the Ku Klux Klan, it can be reasonably anticipated that you are going to get yourself in one helluva mess.

Lem didn't mean that sort of trouble. He was talking about the other kind - that unforeseeable, preposterous and completely undeserved sort of trouble. It stands on the corner watching the world go by. It sees John Schmid and, for no apparent reason, says: "I think I'll give that guy some trouble." So what happens? Something like this:

John sees a meter maid writing out a ticket and notices the car between him and the lady cop is also over-parked. Being a good hearted guy, he reaches into his pocket for some change, planning to feed the meter and do a good deed for some unknown auto owner. A penny drops from his hand.

At this moment, Charlie comes tapping down the sidewalk. Charlie is "tapping down the sidewalk" because his eyes are exceptionally weak and he uses a white cane to help him detect obstacles that might otherwise cause him trouble.

Schmid bends over to pick up the penny. As Charlie is waving his cane around, its tip comes into contact with Schmid's south end. This comes as a surprise to Schmid. He leaps forward, throwing a handful of coins into the air. Unfortunately, the meter maid has finished writing the citation. She turns and starts toward Schmid as he attains the zenith of his leap.

The result is unmitigated trouble. Schmid and the meter maid end up on the sidewalk. Schmid's wife comes out of the drug store in time to see them entangled in a curious position. She has always unjustly suspected him of infidelity and this daylight attack is the final straw. She runs to the nearest lawyer's office and files for divorce.

Charlie, still waving his cane around and puzzled by all the screaming and confusion, falls smack on top of Schmid and the lady cop, thereby making Schmid the butt of a number of Lucky Pierre stories.

Schmid loses his handful of change

The meter maid swears out a complaint charging Schmid with assault of a police officer, attempted rape and overtime parking.

Charlie sues Schmid for damages on account of the bruises and contusions he receive in the scuffle.

Schmid's defense of contributory negligence for failure to

exercise a proper look out fails and Charlie gets an award large enough to buy a seeing eye dog, which promptly bites Schmid in the leg.

You see, trouble of terrible proportions can be visited upon you, any day, any time and without regard to your innocence. Sometimes, if you're fast on your feet, trouble can be outsmarted. As I said, Lem Wright is a wise man and he's able to do it. I'll give you an example.

Lem was preparing his cabin for the deer season a few years ago. Trouble looked in through the window and decided to visit him. Lem got a toothache. Lem took some toothache medicine. It got better. So, Lem took another shot of toothache medicine.

After a period of repeated dosages, the medicine really took hold and Lem started humming to himself. He moved the offending tooth around with his finger and gave serious consideration to the entire matter. He knew he's sober up in the morning. Then the tooth would begin to hurt again. He decided to remove it. Lem wiped off a pair of needle nosed pliers and took some more medicine. One good yank did the trick. Was this all good clean fun with an insignificant potential for trouble?

Not by a jug full.

No sooner had Lem performed the extraction than the enormity of his trouble occurred to him. In one week, Doc Stelter, a dentist friend of long standing, would come to hunt with him. When the Doc noticed the empty space in Lem's mouth, there was no way in hell he would believe anything except that his buddy had gone to another dentist to have his tooth pulled.

The scene was set for losing a good friend and fouling up an entire deer season. Lem, however, finessed around the impending disaster. He wrapped the tooth in a twenty dollar bill and sent it to Doc Stelter together with a note explaining what had happened and apologizing for the attempt to cheat him out of his fee.

And peace and harmony attended them throughout the hunt.

Bear Story

There is more unadulterated bull roar written about the bear than about any of our other furry friends. People appear to be particularly anxious to accept as absolute fact any absurd imbecility printed about the animal. This is probably the result of being conditioned to assign human qualities to the family Ursidae. Consider: Fozzy Bear, Yogi Bear, Goldilocks and The Three, etc.

We are told some of the American Indian tribes thought the bear was a kind of brother or reincarnation of some human relative. We are further told they would apologize to the bear before killing it. I'm more than somewhat skeptical about the report. I think it is pure hogwash.

Can you imagine some guy with a spear waking a black bear in its den some March morning? Can you imagine him setting down the spear, putting his arm around the bear and saying something like: "Hey there, old buddy, buddy. You know the winter has been long and cold and the beaver have been few. We're all kind of hungry down at the lodge and we need some meat. I'm sorry about this, but it looks like you're it"?

If the bear were anything like What's-Her-Name when she wakes up, it would be very dangerous to get too close until after the first cup of coffee. I suspect a bear, being awakened from a nice hibernation, might be a bit testy. I think the bear would give the guy a backhander that would propel him into the middle of next week.

If that legend recounted an apology made after the bear was killed, I might be able to buy it. Anthropologists apparently accept the 'apology' thesis without question. It just goes to show that people are willing to believe any sort of twaddle about the bear. Fact and fiction merge and all kinds of preposterous rot will be considered to be four-square gospel.

You all know I have established an unblemished reputation for reporting the truth, the whole truth and nothing but the truth. To avoid the possibility of even inadvertently writing anything that might result in an accusation of falsehood, fable or fantasy, let me assure you the facts reported herein were very carefully investigated.

I knew Floyd Meyer for over thirty years. We hunted and fished together. One fall, we managed to stay out of jail in Upper Michigan. He told me about one of his own experiences with bear. During the time of our friendship, I am convinced, he told me the truth on more than one occasion and, therefore, I don't doubt the accuracy of his story.

A few years ago, during the deer season, Floyd was hunting in the Nicolet National Forest. It was one of those gray, quiet, not-too cold days. Two or three inches of the white stuff had fallen during the night. It was a good tracking snow.

After an hour or so on a morning stand, Floyd liked to get up and move around a bit. He'd wander off on a mile-wide loop in the hope of jumping a buck or driving one past a stander or just for the simple pleasure of a walk in the winter woods.

Floyd was interested in bears. He liked bears. He liked to see them in the wild. He liked to read about them. He developed a true appreciation and admiration for the beast and he claimed they are very smart. (There are studies that show the IQ of the dumbest bear is higher than the IQ of the smartest state Assemblyman.)

Well, Floyd was on one of his walks and he came upon a set of fresh bear tracks, bigger than your hand. He started following them and knew the animal wasn't far ahead. The tracking was easy in the new snow and they led Floyd to a huge white pine tree. It must have had a ten foot diameter. After following the tracks around the tree, Floyd found himself looking at two sets of bear tracks and only one set of his own. It occurred to him something peculiar was happening.

As he paused to consider the matter, the bear finished its second trip around the tree. It came up behind Floyd and hit him squarely between the shoulders with one of those out-sided paws.

Floyd went sprawling and when he got up to survey the situation, he saw the bear had picked up his 30-06 deer rifle and was pointing it straight at his navel. Surprise turned to terror when the bear slammed a shell in the chamber, raised the rifle and aimed it at Floyd's head.

* * * * *

I prefer a good factual story like that one rather than some of the claptrap printed in magazines and zoology texts. The books tell us the bear is solitary, quarrelsome and omnivorous. I looked that word up and it means the bear will eat anything. The books also tell us the bear has five toes on each foot. I know cats and dogs have only four toes on each foot because I've counted them.

Now, I ask you, who is going to believe the allegation that bear have five toes? Who is going to walk up to a large animal that wants to be alone, is petulant and ill-tempered to an extraordinary degree and will eat anything and then try to count its toes? It's like I'm telling you, you shouldn't believe everything you read about bear.

And another thing. We're told the black bear and all bear cubs can climb trees, but mature grizzlies can't because of their longer and straighter claws. That's a helpful bit of information. However, if I get chased by a bear, I'm not going to stop and try to figure out the age and species of my pursuer. Besides, I'm not so sure I can climb a tree. You do whatever you want. I'm running.

* * * * *

Floyd Meyer managed to extricate himself from the predicament facing him at that large white pine tree. There was only one way to do it. Faced by an angry male holding a rifle, Floyd married his daughter and escaped with his life.

I understand the liaison worked out quite well. His wife doesn't go to the city on shopping sprees or haul him off to cocktail parties and other social engagements. She's kind of growly in the mornings, but that's not uncommon with any of our wives, isn't it?

Floyd had to give up bear hunting. Now he goes fishing instead. It seems he and his wife spent their honeymoon visiting her relatives on Kodiak Island in Alaska. They got him interested in salmon fishing. Floyd wrote to me about it. They don't use rods or reels or flies or bait of any kind. Floyd says their system works very well if you've got fast paws and don't mind sitting in the middle of a stream.

Surviving in the Wilderness
or How to Outlive the Camp Cook

If you review the Tables of Contents of the outdoor magazines at the corner newsstand, you'll find a number of feature articles and columns devoted to the preparation of fish and wild game. Recipes abound for such exotic affairs as Roast Breast of Duck Flambe, Venison Loaf in Sour Cream and Trout with Wine Aspic.

The articles usually contain richly colored photographs of the finished products. They are attractively laid out on mahogany tables with lace table cloths. Fine linen and bone china are scattered about. There may be lit candles.

The dinner table in my cabin doesn't look like that. My table doesn't wobble. It has a shingle under its challenged leg. The surface isn't exactly flat. It has a three degree starboard list. Liquids don't form unsightly pools on it. We make the coffee spillers sit on the low side.

The only table cloth I have is plastic and usually is used to cover something that should be protected from the rain that drips though the ceiling. The dishes and crockery are older than the cabin and four antique dealer are after the silverware.

I suspect those cooking articles are published in outdoor journals because the editors like to see some printed text separating the pages of advertisements. The magazine recipes haven't had any positive effect on the quality of the food served in the woods. You and I both know the grub dished up in most of the deer, fish and bird camps should be labeled by order of the Surgeon General as dangerous to your health.

The continued well-being of the people belonging to the hunting and fishing communities is threatened more by the camp cook than by the anti-gun lobby, the Department of Natural Resources or the pseudo-ecologists. If the truth were known, most of the accidental gunshot deaths occurring during the deer hunting season would be proved to be thinly disguised executions of the camp cook. Heart attacks on trout streams are usually mis-diagnoses of super acute gastric distress brought about by some heavy-handed, incompetent camp chef.

Frankly, Scarlet, most of us don't give a damn about a recipe for Roast Burgundian Moose. We would, however, break out with shouts of "Hossanah" if we could find an article that would teach the cook how to tell the difference between buckwheat flour and white flour that has been frequently visited by mice.

Exposing the camp chef to exquisite game recipes with the expectation of him producing better meals is, at the very best, a forlorn hope. Our time and effort, I believe, would be better spent in teaching our young how to survive the camp kitchen. It's a jungle in there.

Those who are uninitiated in the ways of the camp cook are insensitive to the signs of impending culinary disasters. They will race blindly into a breakfast of scrambled eggs and shells, bacon burned on one side and so raw on the other that ingesting trichinella spiralis is a real possibility - all of this washed down by coffee so strong you can bounce an iron wedge off it.

We, the cognoscente, having noticed the cook mixing burgundy, beer and brandy during the previous night's relaxations, would no more eat the food he prepared for breakfast than we would accept an invitation to lunch with

Lucretia Borgia.

If we want the youngsters to have a fighting chance to live long enough to attain hunting camp old curmudgeon status, we'd better give them the benefit of our advice and counsel, to wit:

1. It is usually a good idea to keep and eye on the cook at meal time. If he avoids a dish, he knows something you don't know. Don't take any of it.

2. Always be sure the dishes have been scalded after washing. Too many hunts have been spoiled by an outbreak of the Mexican Quick Step.

3. Good single malt scotch whisky kills germs, if taken internally and liberally.

4. If there's no tea strainer in the camp kitchen and no grounds in the coffee, make sure the cook is using a clean sock to strain it.

5. Usually, camp cook pancakes are suitable for patching waders or replacing loose linoleum tile.

There are other rules, some of them obvious, like: Never associate with a camp cook in public. The Lycanthrophy Study Section of the University of Chicago Department of Sociology investigated the work histories of Upper Great Lakes camp cooks and reported 31% were people who couldn't make it as drug peddlers, 28% were parolees for hospitals for the criminally insane, 23% were child molesters, 16% were liberal politicians and 8% were book publishers. (NOTE: University of Chicago Sociologists can't add to 100.)

Even though camp cooks are unkempt, surly and not to be trusted near the church poor box, be careful what you say to them. They tend to be a sensitive and short tempered lot. Even mild criticisms, like what they can do with their pot roast, may be met with an enthusiastic attempt to commit bread knife acupuncture.

But let's be fair about it. In spite of their lack of taste and slovenly, boorish ineptitude, the camp cook is a necessary element of our avocations. Theirs is not an easy row to hoe. They have no friends. Their credit ratings are bad. Their lives are constantly being threatened because they forget to put the bay leaves in the bouillabaisse.

Perhaps, we should forgive their defects in character.

Camp cooks are hard to find.

It's a dirty job.

Someone has to do it.

Charlie's Story about the Carp

A bunch of us were sitting around in camp last fall. It was the Thursday before the opening day or deer season, so it was permissible to test the quality of the bourbon, scotch whisky, beer and dry sherry. I suppose that word should be "or," not "and." Free handed drinking is not condoned in Emery Ansorge's camp. There's no imbibing at all on Friday evening. That's when the remaining members of the crew will have driven up from the city after a full day's work. They'll be tired and we'll be rising early on Saturday. So, no libations on Friday. Thursday? Well, that's another matter.

Some of us get to the cabin on Wednesday afternoon. Then we have extra time to check out the territory, find and remove any trees that fell on the trail and get adjusted to deer camp. On Thursday evening, we sit around, pre-testing the quality of the liquids and talking about the sorts of things deer hunters talk about as they await the opening of the season.

We talk about the meal, probably trout or grouse. We have a good camp cook. We talk about what transpired during the day, the work to be done tomorrow and who forgot to sight in his rifle. And then someone says: "Do you remember . . . ?"

Of course, you remember. You may have been there when it happened. If you weren't, you've heard the story at least once a year since 1988. Certainly, you remember. You may not have thought about it for eleven months, but you remember.

In Emery's camp, everyone can tell a story and everyone does. No, that's not right. In Emery's camp, no one can tell a story and everyone tries. It's the same thing. Somebody begins a story . . . "about the time Floyd . . ." and everyone else interrupts, tells the next part of the story or starts off on some tangential tale which someone else interrupts, tells the next . . . and so on.

Everyone gets into the act. Two and sometimes three dialogues go on simultaneously. In the entire history of the camp, no one has been known to express two consecutive thoughts without interruption. It's a rare occasion when there aren't at least two interfering comments punctuating each of the storyteller's sentences.

Picture six men in flame orange shirts, all carrying on separate and interchanging conversation at the same time. There's a grand opera quality about it. It's a deer camp version of the sextet from Lucia di Lammermoor. A tape recording, edited to eliminate the overlaid speech would transcribe something like this:

"Do you remember the time Floyd..."

"Yah, sure. I remember. The deer took a jump to the side and Floyd kept following . . ."

"You need a beer, Russ?"

"Sure."

"He'd probably still be walking around that hill if Emery hadn't come . . ."

"I remember. Emery showed him there were two sets of deer tracks and three . . ."

"Gig, Where's the flashlight. I gotta find my way to the outhouse."

"Those damned deer are damned clever."

"On the table at the door. I think we're storing the caramel corn out there. It'll be on the shelf next to the Sear and . . ."

"Sure they are, but they're deer three hundred and sixty

five days out of the year. We come up here . . ."

"Roebuck catalogue..."

". . . for a week and try to outsmart them. They got all the advantages, and they . . ."

"That's because they know the territory. Let me get a buck into the court room and I'll make him look silly. I'll run rings . . ."

"Every deer crew should have a lawyer in it. I was going to say 'an honest lawyer', but they are so very rare . . ."

"Hah! An honest lawyer couldn't help any of you. You'd need a real crooked . . ."

"Well, you remember Charlie? He sure could have used one."

"Charlie told me a story about a carp and a wallet. I think it was true. It seems . . ."

"On the other hand, I don't believe anyone could prove he ever told the truth - at least, not on purpose."

"How long has Charlie been dead?"

"About ten years."

"You know what they put on his grave stone? Here lies a democrat and an honest man."

"Buried two people in the same grave, did they?"

"Anyway, Charlie like to carry his wallet in his shirt pocket. He was on the Wolf River one spring when the walleye were running ..."

"I understand he was an accomplished after dinner speaker."

"Who? Charlie?"

"Sure. When dinner was over and the bill came, he always managed to be speaking to someone on the telephone . . ."

"Yah. Charlie had deep pockets and short arms."

"He was tighter than the bark on a paper birch tree."

"I had a dog that said 'Birch, Birch.' It was the only bark it knew."

"I don't have to put up with this."

"You better make amends and bring everyone another drink."

"O.K. Yours was the water?"

"There was some scotch in it, too."

"The wallet popped right out of Charlie's shirt pocket and sunk into . . ."

"Speaking of carp, Emery, whatever happened to that old hound dog you used to have up here?'

"I gave him away. There's a story behind it. Last February . . ."

"Is it snowing yet?"

"You need another beer, Russ."

"Sure.

And so it goes. It gets later and later. The story about Charlie and the carp finally gets told. I never heard it before. It's hilarious. The testing continues. We all know it's time to turn in when someone says: "I'll never forget old what's-his-name."

Cabins and Places

Some time ago, some terrible ass from Harvard - I think he was a professor - began appealing for the general use of what he called "mind expanding" drugs. He was talking about LSD, pot and the like. The purpose, I am told, was to develop a state of personal serenity in an otherwise confused existence. Well, I suppose a few years at Harvard is enough to make anyone's mind go soft.

The value of becoming tranquil through a program that destroys the five senses, somehow, escapes me. It's so obvious that tranquility and reality can co-exist. Granted, there is a mighty and pressing need to retreat into a cocoon of peace and tranquility simply because the world has gone mad.

It has, you know. At least, that part able to talk has, largely, become lunatic. Take a look at life in any city with a population of over 50,000. Read a newspaper. Sentence yourself to a full day of television. Listen to a politician. I turn on my heel, walk away from the jury box, and rest my case.

The trouble is, some people don't know how to get away from the foolishness of their day-to-day lives. They have to resort to destructive chemicals. There are many other sane alternatives. Personally, when the cares of the day and the troubles of the world close in on me and threaten to cause angst, I find the raveled sleeve of care is most quickly knit by few days in the cabin.

Now, mind you, I said "Cabin", not "Place". Cabins are different from Places. If you are invited to someone's Place in the woods, you may be assured it is heated by gas, oil or electricity. A Cabin is heated by a stove made of a 55 gallon steel drum. If filled with wood at eleven in the evening, it is cleverly designed to stop operation early enough to cool things down nicely for the first one out of bed in the morning.

A Place can be reached by a passable highway during any month of the year. A Cabin is located at the end of a two rutted trail. It is unused and unusable by automobiles from the end of November to the first of May, thereby giving it ample opportunity to plan how to thwart its owner's annual springtime attempt to drain and make it quasi-passable during the next seven months.

The birds at Places are different from those who frequent Cabins. A Place has Cardinals, Rose Breasted Grosbeaks, Ruby Throated Hummingbirds and Eastern Woods Pee Wees. A Cabin has Camp Robbers and a Downy Woodpecker that tries to knock the hell out of the south side of the building at 6 a.m. every morning.

A Place is clean, or at least reasonably clean. A Cabin wouldn't pass the health inspection rules that governed 18th century London's Gin Alley.

Deer and Raccoon are common around Places because the land surrounding Places has been husbanded in a manner calculated to attract them. If you like animals and togetherness is your bag, then you are a Cabin person because Cabins themselves contain wild life. Weasels? Occasionally. Porcupines? Too often. Mice? Certainly.

Art Meyer allowed a pine snake to make its home in his cabin. It was his way of keeping the mice population under control. There isn't a single mouse in my cabin. They're all married and have big families.

You can usually tell if it's a Cabin or a Place by its name. Guess which one has running water Our Cozy Corner or The Bear Paw? Which one has a complete set of dishes Pine Haven or The Wood Tick Motel? Which one has the outdoor privy where you can read the Sears & Roebuck corset ads: Sylvan Retreat or The Sliver Cat?

Occasionally you'll be fooled. Porcupine Hill has a vacuum cleaner, water comes out of a faucet in the kitchen and the outhouse is built right inside the main building. Kubla Khan may have built a pleasure dome there, but the Xanadu I know was destroyed by carpenter ants. They finished eating it two days before the Town Board voted to soak it in kerosene and put the torch to it in order to protect the rest of the local citizenry from the plague.

My all-time favorite cabin name adorns a log building on the Pine River. It is called, optimistically I fear, The Ascending Angels.

There are signs that will unmistakably identify Cabins. They can be found on Cabin doors. They say things like:

NOTICE - Please don't break the window. The bottom panel of the door is loose. Push it in and reach up to unlock the doorknob. There's nothing worth drinking or stealing in here.

-or-

FRED - I've gone to town for supplies and will be right back. Keep your vicious attack dog, BRUNO, tied up so he won't come after me when I return. PETE

That sign might fool some city felon, but anyone who has worn out a pair of boots will see the paper is weather-beaten and will know the sign has been nailed to the door, winter and summer for at least two years.

Most men like Cabins. A goodly number of them will leave hearth and home and wife and children for a chance to sit in the woods, far from the madding crowd. Women usually prefer Places.

One of the peculiarities of the female of the species is their inconsistency. They enjoy listening to the pit-a-pat of the falling rain when the sound comes from the roof. When it comes from water dripping through the roof and into the coffee can next to the wood box, their enthusiasm disappears completely.

If you are trying to lure some young lovely to your out-of-doors retreat, you are well advise to refer to it as you "Place in the woods". She'll treat an invitation to your "Cabin in the woods" with the same eagerness she'd show for heroin addiction, leprosy or being placed on the rack.

Last year, I thought it would be a good idea to get What's-Her-Name out of the house and show her a good time. I suggested we spend the weekend in my cabin. We could relax, patch the outhouse roof and clean out the mousetraps.

Well, for a moment I thought she suddenly came down with a bad case of hydrophobia. She turned pale and began to foam at the mouth. Her eyes rolled around in an alarming manner and she started to gurgle and make strange sounds. When I tried to give her mouth-to-mouth resuscitation, she bit me.

Suffice it to say she vetoed the idea with all the delicacy and grace of a charging water buffalo. At times, What's-Her-Name is easily excitable. When she's in one of those moods, it's unhealthy to tarry too long. I ran to the four-wheel drive, made my escape and hid out in the cabin until the scare was over.

When I returned on Sunday evening, she had regained her composure and her sense of perspective. She was temperate, serene and her usual, affable self. It's like I say, when I spend a weekend in my cabin, it can do wonders.

Chapter Five

What to Do 'Til the Vernal Equinox Arrives

What to Do 'Til the Vernal Equinox Arrives

The clock and the calendar, unknown in the world of the so-called lower animals, are the masters of our lives. They tell us when to eat - whether we are or are not hungry. They tell us when to go to bed - whether we are or are not sleepy. They tell us when we can fish and when it's all right to chase pheasants or deer.

When an animal is hungry, it eats. When it is tired, it sleeps. It doesn't give a tinker's dam what time it is. It wouldn't think of going to work when it is raining or snowing. It hasn't created a caste of animal politicians to tax it, or animal lawyers to sue it, or animal economists to publish reports calculated to scare hell out of it. Animals are a lot smarter than we are. Some time around December, raccoon and bear and opossum turn down their thermostats and take a nice long rest. They wake up in the spring when the weather is more merciful.

When winter approaches, some Homo sapiens elect to remain more or less awake and busily occupied in doing a number of cold and icy snow season endeavors. Why? Even Koko the gorilla knows there is nothing to do between the end of deer season and the beginning of the trout season. Of course, Koko has an IQ of 4, which, apparently, is higher than that of outdoor type folks who like to frolic in the snow.

I know there's a late grouse season and rabbits can be

hunted and you can run a trap line in January. All of those activities, however, have to be performed when one is up to one's pistol pocket in snow and ice. In my lexicon, any avocation requiring one to freeze or seriously chill the bottom portion of one's anatomy translates into English as: Nothing to do.

If we were as smart as an animal, after butchering the deer and wrapping the venison for the freezer, we'd all hibernate or enter into a pupa stage until the coming of spring. We are not that smart.

December. January. February. March. We travel through those four months like the Ancient Mariner sailing through the Sargasso Sea. It's a painfully slow passage and we are forced to engage in unimportant and miscellaneous matters while we impatiently await the occurrence of the Vernal Equinox. Well, what can we do to distract ourselves from the brooding that comes with the knowledge that it will be another four months before the ice is out and the water heats up to the trout's optimum feeding temperature?

A number of our friends commit ice fishing during this season. They insist it is great fun and, in the places where it is not officially recognized as a felony, they regularly engage in the practice. They claim the addiction has no hold on them, that they only do it socially and that they can stop any time they want to. I doubt it.

I tried ice fishing only once. It didn't do a thing for me. I never chopped a hole large enough to cast my fly into. The hatch was nothing to speak of. (It would be three sentences in a row if I could think of a preposition to end this one with.) Somehow, I can't develop any enthusiasm for a kind of fishing which, as a condition precedent to its enjoyment, requires the ability to play Schafskopf or Pinocle.

Cross country skiing, playing duck calls to the

accompaniment of hard rock CDs and the obsessive chasing of gray squirrels from bird feeders - as well as ice fishing - are all wintertime enterprises invented by sportsmen who became demented by the lack of proper hunting or fishing activity and the failure of their attempts to hibernate.

The months between November and April are the time when the outdoorsman undertakes matters which, at best, are only peripherally associated with hunting and fishing. The more erudite of the fraternity (i.e. those who can read without moving their lips) may disappear into libraries and study entomology, or mushrooms or weather predicting.

Those few who have mastered higher mathematics sometimes spend the winter trying to learn to count to a hundred using the government's waterfowl point count system. The masochists watch television or read the newspapers which have piled up on the front porch since the opening day of fishing season. Everyone has to find a way to avoid rampant cabin fever.

The fly fishermen have the easiest time of it. Tying flies keeps them occupied. It saves them a lot of money, too. This doesn't mean fly tiers don't buy custom built flies each and every spring. They do. They throw away all of their winter production and, just like the rest of us, visit the fly shop every spring to replenish their supplies of Royal Coachmen, Hair Winged Adamses, Rat-Faced McDougals, etc., etc. Their December-to-March occupation of tying flies saves them money by keeping them out of the taverns.

Most of the flies tied by trout fishermen are ludicrous. Still, I suppose they could be effective producers. If a trout saw them, it might die laughing and, belly up, float to the surface where it could be easily netted.

Winter is not a pleasant time for most of us. December isn't so bad, but we become restless in January. In February, symptoms of manic depression begin to appear. In March we are no longer responsible for our actions. Juries regularly acquit sportsmen who commit felonies in March.

As April approaches, we begin to wonder if our four wheel drive vehicle might be able to traverse the two rutted road that leads through the woods, past the swamp and up to the cabin. It can't, but we're apt to try it anyway.

We read the new volumes of government hunting and fishing regulations and try to translate them into comprehensible English. We review and re-stock the contents of our tackle boxes. We begin to think of morel. All of such doings are symptoms of that virulent disease commonly called "cabin fever".

Drug companies have spent millions and haven't been able to develop an effective antidote. When it strikes, no kind of stop-gap activity will move our minds from the woods and the lakes and the streams. Knowledgeable doctors prescribe a weekend in a cabin. It will help, but the only known cure is the advent of the Vernal Equinox.

The Rites of Winter

There comes a time in a man's life when he has to take stock. I don't mean in the sense of a cattle rustler. I mean when he confronts himself, counts his accomplishments and compares them with the aims and aspirations of his youth. It is not always a cheerful occasion.

I recall watching this unhappy process some years ago. I was discussing the cares of the day and the troubles of the world with an older hunting companion. It was November. We were in deer camp. We were reviewing the quality of the contents of a cask of The Macallan late one Friday evening.

Since his youth, he told me, it had been his sincere hope and earnest desire to be turned out to stud when he approached his declining years. Upon his failure to attain that noble goal, he adopted a philosophic attitude and had settled for becoming a camp cook.

Periods of self-analysis usually occur during the Winter season. There's enough happening in the field between May and December to keep the outdoorsman bustling about and engaged in endeavors which fully occupy his mind and leave little time for introspection. But when the glow of deer camp has waned and the December solstice has occurred, there simply isn't much to do. Men have gone mad aimlessly drifting in this doldrums between November and April.

Winter is a dry, dull, stale and unprofitable time of year. The scholars tell us ice fishing was invented on January 20, 1947 by a trout fisherman when he became unbalanced by the prospect of not being able to wet a line until the arrival of Spring. Some sportsmen take their minds off it all by attempting to find out what transpired in the world since their attention was distracted by the previous May opening of the fishing season.

Was there an election? Who won the pennant? What the hell ever happened to the half-back position? Did any catastrophes occur during the summer?

Most catastrophes happen when hunters and fishermen are bored. They happen when the woods, the lakes and the trout streams are frozen. Pearl Harbor happened on December 7th. The National Prohibition Enforcement Act went into effect in January of 1920. It was in January that Fidel Castro took over Cuba, effectively limiting one's ability to find good Havana cigars.

One February, I tried to avoid boredom by organizing a band. I managed to get a string section together, but couldn't find anyone to play a reed or a percussion instrument and my brass section was limited to two saxophonists. I made a video tape of the group and sent it to the local TV station. It was rejected. They sent it back to me, claiming there was already too much Sax and Violins on television.

But try as the sportsman may, sooner or later the ennui and the tedium of this wearisome season will overtake him and he will find himself becoming morosely contemplative - and taking stock. One of the more common Rites of Winter consists of this review of one's past.

Who, among us, has not, while under the melancholy skies of a February, looked back over his life to identify the misbehaviors, the derelictions of domestic duties and the deviations from rectitude he may have committed in the pursuit of his outdoor sport? After that most conscientious and scrupulous review - finding no such derelictions, deviations or misbehaviors - who among us has not, nevertheless, had the vague feeling that somehow he might have done better?

Our wives put up with more than a normal portion of nonsense. What with the preparation of pre-dawn meals, the patching of waders, the de-fleaing of dogs, the plucking of ducks and the like, we should exert ourselves to try to understand and sympathize with their occasional mild complaints. We really should do something nice for them. It would be a pleasant way of saying: "I'm sorry, hon, for any inconsiderate act I may have unwittingly committed during the past year."

I certainly want to show my appreciation for the understanding What's-Her-Name has shown me. Come next Thanksgiving, I'm going to send her to Minneapolis to visit her sister, Darth Vador. Last Thanksgiving, Darth and her children came to visit us. I had to come back in the middle of the deer season to spend the holiday at home with them. I would have preferred to have been back in camp. Hell, I would have preferred to have been tortured by the Apaches and staked out over a hill of fire ants.

Any serious backwards review of a sportsman's life must focus his attention on one area in which almost everyone can use some improvement. You don't spend enough time with your kids and you know it. That son of yours is growing up. Sooner than you think, he will have gone to establish his own life and without the full benefit of your advice and instruction. You will have lost the opportunity to mold his character and give him the solid fatherly guidance that will help him avoid the pitfalls that often ensnare youth.

If you think we're not negligent in the parental advice department, just think of all the young men who get married in June - at the very height of the Hexagena hatch. It's tragic. In the years to come, they will be forced to celebrate wedding anniversaries instead of catching trout.

Every sportsman father should instruct his son to marry during the last week of December. He'll get two income tax exemptions for that entire year. He'll get away with one present for both Christmas and the nuptial anniversary. Moreover, its celebration will not impinge on any worthwhile outdoor event. When January and February are upon us and the world seems deplorably gray, I suppose we all should calmly and dispassionately search out our defects and imperfections, however few and minor they may be, and determine to change - to truly exert ourselves to become more considerate, refined and better men in the coming year.

But take heart. Each day the sun will rise and set a bit further to the north. With any luck, when sunlight and darkness are again in equal balance, we will have completely forgotten all those unspeakable resolutions for self improvement and those gothic fantasies brought on by a morose and monotonous season.

Be Prepared

I don't want to appear to be an alarmist, but I have it on pretty good authority than the world is coming to an end. Well, maybe not actually coming to an end, but don't be surprised if you wake up one of these mornings and find disaster, ruin and grossly deplorable conditions assaulting you from every quarter. And I don't mean just what they do to us in Washington D.C.

If you don't believe it, take a good look in any bookstore. You can buy books that will warn you about the chaos that will follow the impending world-wide financial collapse. Others explain the disaster that will occur when the West Coast slides into the Pacific Ocean. Others explain the disaster that will occur if the West Coast does not slide into the Pacific Ocean. Belligerent visitors from outer space, say some, will do most of us in. You can take your pick. Personally, I prefer the one that claims a new strain of Asian Flu will wipe out almost all humanoids and the squirrels will take over the earth.

When cornered, the experts in the disaster field will admit there is a chance calamity will miss us. Nevertheless, there are a lot of people who are going to be downright disappointed if germ warfare, natural cataclysm, atomic catastrophe and/or the direct intervention of a wrathful Jehovah don't make things really tough on the unprepared.

The people who can clearly foresee the terrible events that will enfold in the next five to ten years don't merely cry havoc. They tell us how to prepare for the coming of their favorite ordeal. For instance, we are advised to eschew investment in stocks and bonds. We should, instead, invest in silver bullion and in gold coins in small denominations. (I notice, however, those same authors have no reluctance to accept paper money in payment of the royalties earned on their books and pamphlets.)

Some writers disclose which parts of the country might miss some of the fallout when China, North Korea, Iraq, Iran, or possibly Paraguay decides to ICBM us. Others tell us where to hide to avoid the destruction following the melting of the polar ice caps and the flooding of the continents. Almost all of them tell us what items should be included in the standard survival kit.

No home, we are warned, should be without a substantial cache of preserved foodstuffs. Those of us who have a good supply of dried prunes will be eating high off the hog while the others will be starving because the power plant went kaput and the electric can opener wouldn't work. Unprepared city dwellers will be trampled to death on the bridge leading out of town while the rest of the unprepared will be scrounging around the countryside, shooting one another.

I've studied the lists of the supplies recommended for the appropriate stocking of every well established sanctuary. I can tell you, friends, life won't be all beer and skittles for those who follow their advice. In my opinion, nobody could last for more than a couple of weeks on the junk included in their inventories. The real essentials for survival have been omitted.

I ask you, who but a complete twit would expect a man to survive the holocaust without a fly rod and a supply of graphite blanks. When the world's monetary system has crashed down around us, terror reigns in the streets and we are safe and snug in our mountain retreat, hole in the ground, or wherever, the disaster and catastrophe folks seem to think we could survive without a hand cranked victrola and a bunch of Lawrence Welk albums.

Really!

If you want to know about survival, don't waste your time on those books. A much better source of information is readily available to you. Ask yourself this question: If He had not wanted you to be able to live out of them for at least a year, why did God create fishing vests with twenty-one pockets? Simply check the contents of a regular, four-square fly fisherman's vest and be prepared to meet thy doom.

Like the mountain men's rendezvous of the old west, in the spring, fishermen congregate near streams reported to contain trout. It was there that a University of Wisconsin fish biologists sliced open the vests of fly fishermen and studied their contents.

The treatise he subsequently published showed the average vest contained Goop, Monkey Grip and wader patches, rubber cement, part of an inner tube for extra patching material and a waterproof metal box filled with matches. You can always tell a man who has read Jack London's "To Build a Fire". He'll carry at least two waterproof metal boxes filled with matches.

Dry flies, wet flies, streamers, nymphs and terrestrials - enough to outfit the entire membership of the Helena, Montana Chapter of Trout Unlimited - are scattered about in a variety of fly boxes as well as in the back of his vest. The flies are snagged into the back of his vest because he hooked himself many times last year and hasn't yet gotten around to cutting them out.

In a footnote, the author expresses his surprise that only a few Rat-faced MacDougals were found. He recommends them because he heard someone used one to catch a 14 inch Brook Trout on the Peshtigo River a couple of years ago.

Most of the vests contained split shot and other kinds of

sinking devices to take leaders down to the bottom of the stream and there is a plastic dispenser filled with 1.2, 2, 3, 4, 6 and 8 pound test tippet. Other than for towing water skiers, I can't think of a use for that 8 pound stuff, but it might come in handy - and there are six spools in the dispenser, so all of them might just as well be used.

A stream thermometer, a flashlight, extra batteries, a rain jacket, a compass and a handful of pre-tied leader of different weights and lengths appear to be necessary equipment. Crazy Glue is popular and some fishermen carry a dark spot at the upper left-hand breast pocket of their vest. This is the mark of a cigar that got wet last year.

Everyone has Mucillin, bug repellent, both cream and spray, dry fly powder, something bought in Montana called Ed's Gunk and a rubbed decoiler to take the kinks and loops out of the leader. There should be two heavy duty retractor chains. One is attached to the net. The other is tied to a tool which contains: a fisherman's nail clipper, a knife blade, a needle-like instrument used to take knots out of leaders, a screw driver, a scissors, an awl, a finger nail file, a can opener, a bottle opener, a cork screw and, I believe, a shotgun shell reloader.

Another essential is a pair of Polaroid glasses. Old timers whose vision is beginning to deteriorate have a jeweler's eye piece. Both glasses and eye piece are tied to the vest with heavy duty leader material. Now I remember why I carry the 8 pound stuff. Everybody should have some.

A fly rod and at least one extra reel, spools of doubled tapered and weight forward sinking and floating lines of different weights, a .357 mag. or .44 caliber Buntline revolver (in case a bear shows up), a hat with a sheepskin band, some extra fly dope and another waterproof metal box filled with matches completes the basic outfit.

A trout fisherman doesn't have to carry food. In the spring, summer and autumn, he lives on the trout he catches and on the protein from the gnats, mosquitoes and no-see-ums he sucks in and digests while on the streams. In the Winter, he survives on the hope and expectations that arise from his contemplations of the opening day of the next trout fishing season.

Throw the Rascals In

After the deer season ended, Mike Stoychoff was reviewing his hunting equipment and preparing to put it all away until the following November. He discovered his reserve of .308 caliber cartridges was dangerously low. In the event the Martians landed and attacked, he would be able to hold them off for only a few months.

Mike retrieved the morning newspaper from the garbage can, scraped off some of the offensive kitchen dregs and began looking for an advertisement announcing an ammunition sale. As he removed the egg shells from page four, he came across an article which, to his surprise, informed him there had been a national election.

Like most outdoorsmen, Mike's attention had been diverted from such matters ever since the fishing season opened in May. Like most outdoorsmen, the trout, big mouthed bass and walleye, as well as the upland birds and the deer had fully occupied his thoughts during the next seven months. And, of course, like most outdoorsmen, he was disgusted with the hypocrisy and power hungry greed of Washington politicians.

It seems as if they all lose any interest they may have had in performing constructive work after their first term. By that time, their only motivation is an ardent and intense desire to maintain themselves in office. They quickly become accustomed to support any special interest spending bill that comes down the pike. They bank on the well proven axiom that no one will vote against Santa Claus, especially if, in each election, they spend more than ten times their annual salary.

Mike says politics and fish management have a lot in common. After a few years in the stream, trout become cannibalistic and begin to destroy their own young. After a few years in Congress, politicians impose heavy taxes the guy who is working, destroying him in order to pay for their own excesses. So, Mike says "Throw the rascals out."

Mike called the newspaper and asked for the names of those who had successfully fooled the electorate and had retired from honest labor to become an elected official. He wrote their names on a sheet of paper and posted it on the refrigerator door. He did this in order to remind himself who to vote against when the next election date rolled around.

The acute political perception displayed by Mike is by no means uncommon among the members of the hunting and fishing fraternities. They recognize the two-fold dangers facing the Republic are, first, the ridiculous actions of our elected officials and, second, the ridiculous inactions of our elected officials.

The problem of the outdoorsman lies not in his perception, but in his preference to be hunting on the day national elections are held. What would happen if volunteers contacted every person who had bought a fishing license, a duck stamp, a deer tag or small game license and pleaded with them to give up a half day's hunting in November, go to the polls and throw politicians out of office.

If such a program were successful and all politicians were replaced after a single term in office, of course, we could look forward to one Congressional Tweedledee being followed by a Congressional Tweedledum. However, the new Tweedledum has not yet caught the Congressional Disease and may actually perform a few worthwhile services for the electorate.

To be fair about it, there is opposition to the Throw the Rascals Out movement. Some contend it is not in the public interest to remove all politicians from office after only a single term.

The Throw-The-Rascals-Out people disagree. With unemployment being so high, they ask, is it not in the public interest to allow some other untrained, inept and out-of-work scoundrel to have an opportunity for a job as a senator or congressman? The TTRO people point out the replaced politicians will suffer no hardship, what with special monetary gifts from Wall Street and the labor unions, kick backs from employees and contributions for services rendered to the special interest groups, they have enough of money to last their families for a generation or so.

Besides, the removed politico has had the broadening experience of traveling all over the world on taxpayer financed junkets. He or she should be ready to allow some other poltroon the chance to create a sizable increase in the national debt. Yes, others deserve to be on the public payroll. It's the American way.

However, if the annual harvesting of politicians becomes widespread, the anti-TTRO people ask, from whence the next batch of office seekers? Won't we run out of qualified candidates? The TTRO people are not worried. There will always be enough bribe takers, perverts, cocaine sniffers and liars in the general population to replace those who have been tossed out of office.

A more valid objection is voiced by the political scientists. Granted, they all agree, politicians are mountebanks, but don't we run the risk of inadvertently electing an honest man to office - a fisherman, for example? (Fishermen are clearly more truthful than politicians.) The possibility of sentencing some innocent, honest man to Congress where he must associate with liars and thieves, is about the same as giving an innocent man a death penalty sentence.

The TTRO people are willing to make provision to reduce that risk. They propose the appointment of a Special Parole Board composed of respected jurists. After a fair trial, if the Board is convinced the newly elected official is honest, it would have the authority to peremptorily remove him from office and immediately send him home.

For my own part, I am not a TTRO partisan. I believe their movement should be shunned. If taken seriously, its effect on society would be traumatic, to say the very least. There may be widespread appeal to the call "Throw the rascals out", but before we rush to the polls, vote the knaves out of office and force them onto the welfare rolls, let us give some thought to the consequences of our actions.

Where would we throw them? Can you name a Senator you would invite into your deer camp? - a Congressman you would not shoot in the leg if you encountered him while grouse hunting? If a politician loses an election, we all run the fearsome risk of him leaving our national capitol and returning to live in our own communities.

Instead of seeing him only around election time, murmuring, "I'm an environmentalist. I'm an environmentalist," we might have to put up with him every day of the year.

No! No, never. We're much better off keeping him in office, far away in nation's capitol. I say "Throw the rascals in."

Superiority

Ring the banjoes! Give us a drum roll! Set up drinks for the house! We are Homo sapiens. We are the very wisest of the sub-species of the genus we share with the large apes. We are the most intelligent life on the planet with knowledge, judgment and abilities vastly superior to those of our nearest monkey cousins and infinitely transcendent over those winged, finned, four, six and multi-footed creatures who try to share the earth with us.

Do you really think so?

Is mankind truly superior?

Or is his present condition of ascendancy merely the result of the fact of his thumb being placed in a position which enables his hand to grasp a club? Have you ever stopped to consider that the claim of human superiority is only made by the human itself? No other form of life has publicly endorsed it and, at times, even the human being has obliquely recognized his own inferiority.

When, as occasionally happens, one of us shows some good judgment, he is said to have "horse sense". If someone is particularly clever, he is "sly as a fox". He might even be "strong as an ox", "wise as an owl", or "eagle eyed." Now then, have you ever heard the phrase "man sense", "strong as a man", "wise as a man", "sly as a man" or "man eyed"? Of course not.

Still, the Homo sapiens goes around loudly proclaiming his intellectual superiority and, if he hears even a moderate demurrer, he takes up a club and silences the opposition. When the posturing and chest pounding have concluded, if you take a careful and unbiased view of the matter, you may have to conclude the birds and the beasts have long been slandered. It is time they be recognized as the more perfectly designed and intelligent forms of life.

I don't mean just the woodcock, the deer or the small mouthed bass that regularly make a fool out of you. I mean almost any kind of animal. To put it bluntly, is mankind superior to, say, the porcupine? I doubt it. It is well known that porcupines can match the human being in a number of fields of endeavor. Flying by waving the arms and transmuting baser metals into gold come to mind as two examples.

To determine just who is the smartest, I suggest we compare the porcupine to your brother-in-law. Is your brother-in-law as good looking as a porcupine? Is he as energetic and as fast on his feet? Does he have superior mechanical skills?

"Unfair. Unfair," you shout? You believe your brother-in-law is sub-human? - an unfortunate genetic throw back? - not truly representative of the human being? Well, maybe you're right. Let's try another comparison.

The next time you're at the corner tavern, take on too much "big mouth" and incur the extreme displeasure of the 300 pound, eight foot tall truck driver who is standing between you and the door, try this defensive maneuver. As he cocks his fist and advances toward you, quickly turn sideways and whack him with your tail. Unless he happens to be a ballet dancer in disguise, you will soon find yourself in very serious trouble and in need of emergency hospitalization.

A porcupine, finding himself in the same situation, would best his assailant and continue drinking his beer and talking smart.

If you still think you are superior to the porcupine, you

should talk to Steve Gress. Steve has a log cabin on the Tamarack River in Upper Michigan. He and some friends expanded it a few years ago and when the new roof was finished, he took off his gloves, laid them on the top rung of the ladder and slid down to join the rest of the crew in celebrating the occasion.

Some time after three on the following morning, Steve was wakened by a strange noise coming from the new roof. He managed to get himself in a vertical position, find a flashlight and go outside to investigate the cause of the disturbance. According to Steve, a porcupine was sitting on the top rung of the ladder trying to put on one of his gloves.

Some people think the porcupine was simply chewing on the glove to get at the salt that is part of the sweat that runs down one's arm and into one's gloves if one insists upon working on one's roof during the heat of an August afternoon. Other people think the prolonged roof completion celebration may have somehow resulted in impaired vision.

But I digress. The point of the story is: Porcupines can climb ladders as well as people can. People can't climb trees as well as porcupines can.

Steve is convinced porcupines are smarter than people. He speaks with some experience because he developed a close relationship with one of our spiny friends. It all started when Steve was sitting on his porch, admiring the scenery one May morning.

A porcupine shuffled up to him. Steve had some stale soda crackers in the cupboard. They were left over from the previous season's deer camp. He tossed a few at the porky, who licked the salt from them and then wandered off. Steve took to feeding the crackers to the porky as a kind of insurance policy. If it got its salt from the crackers, maybe it wouldn't chew on the outhouse.

The stratagem worked. It also produced a special friendship between man and beast. Otis would waddle into the yard and get his ration of crackers. Then he'd follow Steve around like a puppy dog, softly grunting and mewing. The first time Otis crept up behind him and rubbed against his leg, Steve had a bad case of what has been called "the leaping frights." It soon became evident the porcupine only wanted to be friendly and a bond between man and animal developed.

Otis liked to have his back scratched and Steve regularly performed that service for him - wearing a thick leather glove. The few quills that came loose would stick to it and not to Steve. Whenever a visitor saw the quilly glove hanging near the cabin door, he would inquire of it and Steve would tell him about his friend, Otis the porcupine.

This, says Steve, proves porcupines are smarter than people. While the visitors accepted it as unadulterated fact, no porcupine would ever be taken in by such a ridiculous story.

When Steve knocked it off the ladder, the porky fell to the ground and landed on top of the glove. Steve picked it up and hung it on the cabin door, quills and all.

Predicting the Weather

Most hunters and fishermen watch the ten o'clock news not because they want to learn about the disaster-of-the-day, but because they want to plan the next day's foray into the out-of-doors.

Is a cold front moving down from Canada, chasing the late bluebill before it? Will there be a light tracking snow for the opening day of the deer season? Will a heavy rain flood the river, wash out the bridge and keep What's-Her-Name from driving to Philadelphia on her shopping trip?

In other words, the TV weather forecasters are very important factors in the sportsman's life. We depend upon them - and how do they discharge their responsibilities to us? They treat us with contempt.

The profession of weather forecasting has been the training ground for such proficient perjurers as Baron Munchausen, Joseph Goebbels, Ananias and the members of the United States Senate. The Supreme Court has ruled the testimony of weather forecasters, even when taken under oath, is not admissible in any court in the land. (If they haven't come down with such a ruling, they should do so at once. Television weather forecasters are notorious liars.)

The evening before the opening of the trout season, they assured us the wind would come from the west at 0 - 10 miles per hour, the temperatures would be: "lows in the mid 50s, highs in the mid 60s, partly cloudy with a 25 percent chance of precipitation".

Well, three and a half inches of white, large flaked "partly cloudy" fell on our river raft. Part of it was blown off by the winds of gale force. I couldn't cast a line because it froze into the eyes of my fly rod. The TV forecaster should have done the honorable thing and committed suicide. Hell, he didn't even apologize.

There's a story about an Alaska gold miner who complained that the roulette wheel in the local saloon was outrageously crooked. When asked why he played it, the old timer said: "I have to. It's the only wheel in town." For too long the TV weathermen have been the only wheel in town. It's time we did something about it.

Ever since the painful experience of that opening day, I've dedicated a goodly portion of my waking hours to researching and collecting the time tested rules and traditional maxims that aided our forefathers in making their short and long term hunting and fishing plans. The labors have not been completed, but, so far, they've proven to be as accurate as those jokers on the TV. You deserve a preliminary report, and here it is.

Smoke is a good indicator of near term weather conditions. If smoke comes out of the chimney and falls to the ground, it will rain. If the smoke moves to the west, bad weather is on the way. If it blows to the east, good weather is on the way. These rules are infallible. They have always proved to be 100 percent accurate. Sometimes I've had to wait a few weeks after observing how the smoke moved, but, sooner or later, the predictions were correct.

In the winter, if it is cloudy and the smoke goes straight up, there's a fifty-fifty chance it will snow. The first eight times I saw the smoke rise vertically on cloudy winter days, it didn't snow. That means the next eight time I observe it, it will snow.

There is a problem with the chimney smoke method of forecasting. It requires one to carry a chimney around with him. Rather than hauling a chimney, the outdoorsman is well advised to carry water, brick and mortar. They are less bulky and easier to transport that the pre-built models.

How many times have you gone through a hunting or fishing outing limiting your comments to: "It's hot," or "It's cold?" I suppose you could call the nearest TV station and ask, but they would probably lie to you. If you want an accurate temperature reading at any time, the "Chirping Cricket Rule" will help you. The rule has been used for centuries.

Count the number of chirps made by one cricket in fifteen seconds. Then add thirty-seven. The result will be the temperature. I can attest to the accuracy of the Chirping Cricket Rule. During that trout fishing disaster, I listened carefully and didn't hear a cricket chirp on nine different occasions during the fifteen second period. Guess what? Minus nine, plus 37 equals 28, and that was the exact temperature - 28 degrees.

The CCR produces a Fahrenheit temperature reading. If you happen to be a European and want a Celsius count, it's easy to figure it out. Start with 37. Add the number of chirps in fifteen seconds. Then subtract 32. Then multiple by 9 and divide the result by 5. (Or is it add 32, divide by 5 and multiply by 9?) To be on the safe side, you may want to carry a thermometer.

Rain prediction maxims have been with us for a long time. A heavy morning dew presages a clear weather day, but it will rain if: cow herds lie down in the morning; spiders stay in their webs; the tips of the leaves on hardwood trees turn upwards; soot falls down the chimney; or, you're standing in the middle of a trout stream and have forgotten your rain jacket.

During a rain storm, if you face the wind, your extended right arm will point to the center of the disturbance and your neighbors will point to you as someone without enough brains to come in out of the rain.

For long term forecasting, remember - a "buttermilk sky" (cirro-cumulus clouds and "mare's tails") promise rain in two days. Count the number of stars within the ring around the moon and you'll know the number of days until the next rainfall. On the first day of the first snow, count the number of days to the last full moon. It will snow that many times during the winter. If the first snow stays on the ground for three days, a second snow will cover it.

For every foggy day in August, there will be a day of snow in the winter. The hotter the summer, the colder the winter. If the squirrels build their nests closer to the ground, expect a cold winter. Ditto if there's a heavy crop of berries, acorns and pine cones.

Thunderstorms and tornadoes deserve comment. One of the oldest weather folk adages goes back to the Iron Age. A rough translation from the Sanskrit is: If the wind blows heartily and the sky becomes blackened and fearful thunder occurs in the sky, quickly get rid of your golf club or you may be hit by lightning.

Tornadoes cross the land at a speed of between 20 and 40 miles per hour and, usually, in an east-northeasterly direction, but the wind velocity within the swirling storm may attain 400 miles per hour. Tornadoes occur only in the United States and nowhere else in the world. But then, we're the only country with a Senate and a House of Representatives.

While fishing in northern Canada, I asked the guide to predict the next day's weather. He took a handful of sand and ran it through his fingers. Then he crumpled a maple leaf and smelled it. He looked at the clouds, the moon and the sky. Then he said: "Big wind. Come soon.................. Maybe."

As soon as the story got out, he was hired as a weatherman by a Philadelphia TV station.

The Rites of Spring

George Huebner has a finely constructed log cabin on the North Branch of the Pine River. It has a huge stone fireplace, a sauna and a supply of antiques and old lumberjack carvings. They are used, not just looked at. The natural beauty of the trees and the river, together with a reasonable supply of deer, Ruffed Grouse and Brook trout, create an almost perfect setting.

I say "almost perfect" because you have to cross the river to get to George's cabin. Now, crossing a river is not, in itself, a particularly unpleasant activity. Crossing the bridge to get to George's cabin, however, was an experience that could make courageous men tremble, involuntarily fill their lungs and then hold their breath.

The bridge was probably strong enough. George built it himself with heavy timbers imported from a nearby government forty. George built things right, but I'll admit his bridge sure looked bad. It wasn't so much the chewed up quality of the timber, the warp and 18th century look of the covering lumber or the apparently un-cared-for approach. The bridge leaned to the left. It didn't just lean to the left. I mean the damned thing LEANED TO THE LEFT.

George didn't help any. It was his usual practice, when driving someone to his cabin for the first time, to stop the car when it got to the bridge. He'd get out, look at various parts of the structure and slowly shake his head back and forth. Then he'd cautiously edge out to the center and jump up and down a few times. He'd get back into the car, start the engine, pause, pop the clutch and careen over the bridge. He'd stop on the other side, look at his white faced companion who might still be in a state of shock, and say: "Well, I made it again."

There's a newer bridge there now. The old one fell victim to a spring flood. The new bridge doesn't lean to the left. It even has rails on it's sides. Every April, I drive up to George's cabin. When I cross his bridge over the Pine River, I say to myself: "Well, I made it again." It's one of my rites of spring.

The outdoorsman's rites of spring are apt to be highly individualized acts. They might be described, generally, as seasonal deviations from rational behavior. They renew the spirit. They clean winter's accumulation of rust and scale from the pipes. They keep him from growing old and cruddy. Some of them are planned - like the ritual of the opening day of the trout fishing season. (Same companions. Same river. Caviar. Champagne.) Some, though repeated each year, seem to be set in motion by ancient forces, unknown and uncontrollable.

For example, upon the occurrence of the Vernal Equinox, a strange and inexplicable impulse to clean a cabin in the woods seizes men who, their wives will confirm, are congenitally unable to clean a cellar, a garage or any part of a city house. It is a virulent ailment and the passion increases in intensity until, by mid-April, it can no longer be resisted.

He drives down the (so-called) improved town road and onto the two rutted trail that leads to his cabin. Trail? Hah! In mid - April, it is more closely akin to a poorly maintained otter slide. It's impassable, but the urge is too strong and the spring ritual must be observed.

The 4-wheel drive charges forward and covers about one third of the distance to the higher ground. Then it slides in the slush, sinks to its hub caps, coughs, shudders and resigns. The second act of the scenario consists of the discovery that he has neglected to bring the bumper jack, the axe or the come-along.

He forgot them last year, too.

What's-Her-Name is, invariably, present when I am involved in such a catastrophe. In times of crisis she is always beside me - either making snide comments or being hysterical. The afternoon is spent getting the vehicle back to the town road which suddenly seems as well constructed as the Pennsylvania Turnpike.

Another pagan manifestation of the change of season appears concurrently with the early fungi. The rites of spring include a trip to the book store to buy yet another treatise dedicated to the description and identification of mushrooms. Government statistics prove only 26 out of the 1,358 mushroom book buyers have ever picked a mushroom.

I know of four places to pick morel. One is in town. It's a field where the kids play baseball as part of their rites of spring. The possibility of their deciding to use a group of Morchela Esculenta as third base will give a sane man sleepless nights. Part of my own rites of spring consists of telling them: "Those toadstools are particularly poisonous, kids. Don't get close to them. Don't even kick them. If you do, the poison will get on your shoes and kill your dog."

Last week some fool came past with a lawn mower and destroyed at least three good meals. He didn't recognize the damage done by his outrageous action. I can't tell him about the morel for fear he'll claim them for himself. He might do so, thinking they belong to him just because he owns the field.

I think I've got the problem solved. I've informed the Internal Revenue Service that he is operating a lawn care business and not reporting the income on his tax returns. By next spring he will be languishing in some federal prison rather than mowing down my morel. Serves him right.

When the sap begins to flow in the hard maples and

Andromeda and Pegasus rise in the eastern sky, many a restless night will be spent by fly fishermen, dreaming the impossible dream - that they will develop the ability to fish nymphs. The County Treasurer will again do a land office business selling replacement Sportsman's licenses to those who, once again, lost theirs after the end of deer season. Librarians will be deluged with requests for books containing instruction on how to remove melted chocolate bars from tapered leaders, streamers and fishing vests.

Ah, the rites of spring.

I suppose some people are insensitive to the primordial call of springtime. If you are one of those unfortunates, I invite you to join me. On March 22, I intend to stand before the window, open it, look out, take a deep breath, sigh, and say out loud: "Well . . . I made it again."

Backword

When writing a book, the author begins by assembling a large number of words - thousands and thousands of them. He puts them in a large box. I used the bathtub. Then, one by one, he withdraws them and, with scotch tape or library paste, he attaches them, in nice straight lines, to sheets of paper. The sheets are then shuffled and sent to the printer.

In the case of BACKLASH, when the book was finished, I had used every word except six adjectives and three nouns. With no verbs, adverbs, articles or conjunctions left, they could not be used. They are perfectly good words and should not be swept off the desk top and into the waste basket. They deserve a better fate.

The words left over from BACKLASH are:

ANTHROPOMORPHISM
CRAPULENT
GNOFF
HUBRISTIC
NEOTERIC
OXYMORONIC
PHTHISISIC
PRIAPISTIC
ANTIDISESTABLISHMENTARIANISM

Please use them.

Galen Winter

Other Books by Galen Winter

500 WILD GAME AND FISH RECIPES (Editor)

LEGENDARY NORTHWOODS ANIMALS
A Farcical Field Guide

BACKLASH II
More Tales Told by Hunters, Fishermen
and Other Damned Liars

THE AEGIS CONSIPRACY

THE BEST OF THE MAJOR

THE CHRONICLES OF MAJOR PEABODY

THE JOURNALS OF MAJOR PEABODY

www.ingramcontent.com/pod-product-compliance
Lightning Source LLC
Chambersburg PA
CBHW022025090426
42739CB00006BA/282